D0427044

A GARDEN OF WORDS

ALSO BY MARTHA BARNETTE

The Bill Schroeder Story

MARTHA BARNETTE

A Garden of Words

Illustrated by Dorothy Leech
Calligraphy by Gun Larson

TIMES BOOKS

LIBRARY OF CONGRESS CATALOGING-IN-PUBLICATION DATA
Barnette, Martha.
A garden of words / by Martha Barnette.—1st ed.
p.   cm.
Includes index.
ISBN 0-8129-1848-7
1. Indo-European languages—Etymology—Names.
2. Flowers—Nomenclature.   3. Plant names, Popular.
I. Title.
P769.B37   1992
582.13'014—dc20   91-38733

Jacket illustration by Sergio Baradat

Art directed by Naomi Osnos

Designed by Beth Tondreau Design

Manufactured in the United States of America
3   5   7   9   10   8   6   4   2
First Edition

This book is dedicated to my parents,
Helen and Henlee Barnette,
and to
the memory of
Professor Leonard Latkovski, Sr.
1905–1991

CONTENTS

EXORDIUM   ix

Amaryllis   3

Anthurium   9

Aster   1 8

Chrysanthemum   2 7

Columbine   3 2

Daisy   4 5

Dandelion   5 9

Geranium   6 6

Gladiolus   7 2

Hyacinth   7 9

Hydrangea   8 5

Iris   9 3

Lily   9 8

Loosestrife   1 0 8

Lupine   1 1 3

Nasturtium   1 2 4

Orchid   1 3 3

Pansy   1 4 1

CONTENTS
· · ·

Poppy   149

Rose   157

Tulip   166

Zinnia   174

LIST OF FLOWERS   183

ACKNOWLEDGMENTS   187

EXORDIUM

*E*xordium is a Latin word that was adopted into English to mean "the introduction to a written work." Originally, however, the word *exordium* indicated "the beginning of a web" or "the threading of a loom." In a sense, that's what this book is all about: It begins to weave a web of words and reveals the linguistic threads that link a host of seemingly unrelated words and languages.

This book had its beginnings a dozen years ago, when I was struggling through introductory college Greek. Classical languages are notoriously difficult to master, in part because these so-called "dead" languages don't afford the chance to practice rudimentary conversations—*Hello, How are you?, What's your name?*—and other everyday exchanges that provide a feel for the spoken language. Instead, the first chapter of an ancient Greek or Latin textbook introduces students to such terms as the Greek words for "metaphor" and "bowstring," or the Latin word for "treachery"—not exactly the stuff of everyday conversation. In addition, anyone who wants to learn a classical language faces formidable lists of noun declensions and seemingly endless charts of verb forms.

It all seemed so arbitrary, so artificial, so far removed from real life. Who, I wondered, had decreed that a noun should have so many different endings, depending upon its use in a sentence? How did the ancients ever come to decide that a Greek verb should have three voices, four finite moods, seven tenses, three numbers, six principal parts—and *why*? How, for that matter, did any ancient Greek kid ever learn to carry on a conversation at all? The old expression "It's Greek to me" took on a new and painful meaning, and I finally decided to drop the course and try again the following year.

In the meantime, I wrote to the university in my hometown of Louisville, Kentucky, to ask whether some graduate student there might tutor me in Greek over the summer. I received a letter back—in not entirely perfect English—from someone who said he'd be glad to help. Leonard Latkovski, Sr., was a retired professor of classics who had taught for many years at Louisville's Bellarmine College. He began his teaching career in his native Latvia at the University of Riga. In 1944 he and his young family fled to Germany, just hours ahead of the advancing Russian Army. Eventually they emigrated to the United States. Although now officially retired, Professor Latkovski regularly worked as a freelance translator in several languages, taught Latin in a Catholic elementary school, and tutored adults in the evenings. He agreed to teach me Greek on Monday nights.

The ritual that began our first tutorial would be

repeated in all our subsequent meetings. A portly, gracious man, Professor Latkovski greeted me in modern Greek and kissed both my cheeks. With a grand gesture, he motioned for me to be seated, then disappeared into the kitchen. He returned after a moment with two cups of strong coffee. He left again, returning this time with a loaf of fresh home-made bread. In a heavily accented kind of growl he said, "Recipe from old country. I baked just for you." He left and came back a third time with a plate of butter. "Cow cheese," he said, and went on to explain that English *butter* comes from the ancient Greek words *bous,* or "cow," and *turos,* "cheese"— making *butter* a linguistic relative of such words as *bovine, beef, bucolic,* and *bulimia,* or literally, "ox-hunger."

At last the professor settled into a chair and announced, "*Now* we can study." I had in hand my elementary Greek textbook, full of dreary drills, charts, and written exercises. I was hoping the professor would look over my written work, correct my mistakes, and quiz me on noun forms. The professor tried halfheartedly to oblige, but he was clearly restless. More than once he frowned, shook his head, and muttered, "Language is not arbitrary. There is a reason for it all. Is *not arbitrary!*" As the lesson wore on, the professor repeatedly insisted on digressing from the exercises to talk about words in other languages. I left, quite frankly, disappointed.

The following week the professor announced that

we wouldn't need my textbook anymore. Instead he handed me a copy of Sophocles' *Oedipus the King.* "We will read this," he said with a finality that let me know it was useless to argue. The professor read aloud the first few lines in Greek and translated them into English. Then he sifted through them again, word by word, pointing out subtleties of meaning and linguistic connections between the Greek words and those from other languages.

One of the first words he chose was the name of the title character, Oedipus—or, as the professor tended to call him, 'The Oedipus.'

"The name Oedipus means 'swollen foot.' When 'The Oedipus' was a baby, he was left in the woods to die, so that he would not fulfill the oracle's prophesy that he would kill his father and marry his mother. His ankles were pierced and fastened together, as was the custom in those days. The baby survived, you remember—a shepherd rescued him —and because of his swollen feet he was called 'Oedipus.'

"You have in English, do you not, the word *edema,* yes? Is some sort of medical term that has to do with 'swelling,' yes? It comes from Greek *oidein,* which means 'to swell.' Is also the source of the name 'Oedipus.' "

I started to say something, but he held up a hand. "And that's not all yet. The rest of his name is from the Greek for 'foot,' *pous.* You have it in the word *octopus,* an animal with 'eight feet.' The genitive form of Greek *pous,* which is *podos,* is in such English words as *podiatrist,* or 'foot doctor.'"

The word *podiatrist* reminded him of something else: "The Greek word for 'doctor,' you see, is *iatros* —as in the *psychiatrist* who doctors the *psyche* or 'soul.' You have in English, do you not, the adjective *iatrogenic*? It describes an illness that was generated by the *iatros,* or 'doctor.'" The professor smiled.

"And that's not all yet. From the Indo-European root of Greek *pous* comes the Latin word for 'foot,' *pes,* and its stem *pedis,* as in *pedestrian, pedestal,* and *sesquipedalian.* Is wonderful word, *sesquipedalian.* Literally, it means 'a foot and a half long,' so a word that is *sesquipedalian* is just a really big one! Is terrific word!"

By now the professor could hardly contain his merriment. "And that's still not all yet. In Sanskrit is same thing: The Sanskrit word for 'foot' is *padas,* like Greek *podos* and Latin *pedis.* And Sanskrit has a wonderful word for 'tree,' *padapa.* You know what means *padapa*? The one that 'drinks with its foot.' Is fantastic language, Sanskrit. Very poetic! And that's still not all yet. In Latvian and Lithuanian . . ."

As we made our way through the opening lines of *Oedipus,* nearly every word set the professor off on some etymological romp—dizzying excursions across the boundaries of time, culture, language. Three hours flew by as he discoursed on a vast array of subjects, from ancient botany to modern medicine, folklore to mathematics, history to psychology, alchemy to the periodic table of the elements. By the time I left that evening, carrying another loaf of his homemade bread under my arm, my mind was reeling from the sheer amount and scope of information we'd covered. I couldn't wait to see if the amazing things he told me were substantiated in standard reference works. (Indeed, they nearly always were. Later, for example, I found not only the picturesque Sanskrit word for "tree," *pādapa,* or "the one drinking with its foot," but also the intriguing term *pāda-pôpagata,* which means "abiding under a tree while expecting death.")

At that rate, of course, it took us quite a while to work our way through *Oedipus the King*—seven years, in fact. But what a journey! I began to grasp language with an understanding that charts of declensions and lists of verb forms could never supply. I came to see the common linguistic ancestors that link words in a surprisingly large number of languages—and to realize that, as the professor had insisted, those words and their various grammatical forms were anything but arbitrary.

During the next twelve years, I completed college (taking as many Greek courses as possible), went on to work as a newspaper reporter, and later studied Greek in graduate school. I also continued to meet regularly with Professor Latkovski. Sometimes emergency phone calls interrupted our lessons: A Polish woman who spoke no English was in labor at a nearby hospital. A Romanian family who had just moved to the area was seeking an interpreter. A Turkish woman who had arrived in Louisville for surgery needed a translator. Professor Latkovski was the one to call.

Over the years, I sometimes asked the professor how many languages he spoke; he invariably dismissed the question with a chuckle and a shrug, adding, in all seriousness, "There are many languages I do not know." He was far more interested in how much more there was to learn, always eager for someone to show him a new word. He never did tell me how many languages he knew, although his university colleagues said that he was perfectly comfortable in at least twelve of them, and the library in his home contained dictionaries and lexicons in a total of thirty languages.

In the summer of 1991, as I was completing the final draft of this book and continuing my weekly studies with the professor, he suddenly fell ill. A few days later I awoke with an overwhelming feeling that somewhere a library was burning. A short time later, Professor Latkovski died, just a few weeks before his eighty-sixth birthday.

This book is an effort to capture some of the spirit and substance of what he taught me.

APPROXIMATELY half the world's population speaks languages that arose from a common ancestor. This "mother tongue" was spoken by tribes that eventually spread throughout Europe, to Iceland and Ireland in the west, and eastward to India and what is now part of Chinese Turkestan. Using the science of comparative linguistics, scholars have reconstructed some two thousand fundamental roots that represent this mother tongue, which is known as Indo-European. By analyzing remnants of these roots in various ancient and modern tongues, they have discovered links among English and such diverse languages as Russian, Persian, Danish, Polish, Hindi, Latvian, Spanish, German, Greek, and Sanskrit, as well as those of the ancient Hittites and Tocharians. (A small but growing number of linguists subscribe to the idea that Indo-European itself may be only one branch of a far older tongue, which they call Nostratic, from Latin *noster,* "our." Nostratic, according to this revolutionary idea, is the source of every language in the world. This intriguing hypothesis remains highly controversial among scholars.)

Not a word of Indo-European was ever written down, so how do we know that it, or something like it, existed? The answer is the strikingly consistent correspondence between various features of both classical and modern languages. Among the first to point out such similarities was the English jurist and amateur linguist Sir William Jones, who outlined this idea in his 1786 speech to the Asiatick Society of

Calcutta—a speech now excerpted in almost every introduction to books about word origins:

> ... [T]he Sanskrit language, whatever may be its antiquity, is of wonderful structure; more perfect than the Greek, more copious than the Latin, and more exquisitely refined than either, yet bearing to both of them a stronger affinity, both in the roots of verbs and in the forms of grammar, than could possibly have been produced by accident; so strong that no philologer could examine all the three without believing them to have sprung from some common source, which, perhaps, no longer exists.

These similarities are exactly the kind Professor Latkovski meant when he compared the words for "foot"—Greek *pous,* Latin *pes,* Sanskrit *padas,* and their offspring—all of which descend from that "common source," the Indo-European root now called **PED-1.** Consider also the Indo-European root for "three," **TREI-**: This gave rise to English *three,* Spanish *tres,* French *trois,* Swedish *tre,* Lithuanian *trys,* Albanian *tre,* Bengali *tri,* Russian *tri,* Polish *trzy,* Greek *treis,* Welsh *tri,* and so on. In German this root became *drei,* and in Dutch, *drie,* reflecting a correspondence between *d* and *t* sounds in various languages that we'll see repeatedly in this book. (This correspondence of consonants is also reflected in English *two* and its various cognates[1] in other languages, such as Spanish *dos* and French *deux,* as well as the kindred English word *duo.*) Another such correspondence often occurs with the letters *l* and *r.* For example, the Greek word *polis* or "city"—as in *metropolis,* or literally, "mother city"—arose from the Indo-European root designated as **PELƏ-2**; from this root also came Sanskrit *pur,* "city," now part of the name *Singapore,* or literally, "the lion city."

These types of correspondences among the descendants of Indo-European are described in more detail in Harvard professor Calvert Watkins's introduction to the indispensable *American Heritage Dictionary of Indo-European Roots* (1985), from which much of this book's information on these roots is drawn. Robert Claiborne also provides highly readable discussions of this topic in *Our Marvelous Native Tongue* (Times Books, 1987) and *The Roots of English* (Times Books, 1989). For our purposes here, it's sufficient to understand that these consistent sound correspondences have enabled scholars to open a window on a new and fascinating means of understanding human thought.

THE etymological histories of flower names in this book provide an excuse for talking about the book's

. . . .

[1] A cognate is a related word of similar sound and sense, such as English *mother,* German *Mutter,* and Spanish *madre.*

real subject: language itself. Just as the opening lines of *Oedipus* provided a starting point for Professor Latkovski, each flower name prompts etymological excursions in many surprising directions. A look at the dovelike *columbine* leads to a consideration of the many animals named for their color, including the *opossum,* the *bear,* and possibly the *penguin.* The *gladiolus* inspires a discussion of various types of weaponry, as well as the surprising connections between *algebra* and bone-setting, and between *manicotti* and *manure.* The misunderstood *lupine* flower prompts a look at a number of tales about wolves, plus the faint etymological connection between a certain "wolf-word" and a *tuxedo.*

In fact, these chapters encompass much more than language—they're about history, culture, science, philosophy, literature, and myth. Like the professor's tutorials, each chapter is packed with wide-ranging information. Above all, this book is intended to raise as many questions as it answers—all the better to send you off on wild and wonder-filled etymological romps of your own.

EXORDIUM

· · ·

A GARDEN OF WORDS

Amaryllis

*T*he ancient writers of Latin pastoral poetry often celebrated the natural beauty of a young shepherd woman named *Amaryllis.* The rustic charms of young Amaryllis also proved to be a favorite subject for the English romantic poets. John Milton wrote wistfully of the temptation to "sport with Amaryllis in the shade." This young woman's allure is likewise commemorated by the spectacular trumpet-shaped flower that bears her name—a name thought to derive from the Greek verb *amarussein,* which means to "sparkle," "dazzle," or "scintillate."[1]

The amaryllis flower belongs to the botanical genus *Hippeastrum.* This name is also worth a closer look: It comes from the Greek word *hippos,* meaning "horse," and refers to the fact that a few days before the amaryllis bud opens, the two pointed leaves enclosing it stick up in a way that resembles a horse's ears.

Both Greek *hippos* and its offspring *Hippeastrum*

· ·

[1] *Scintillate* itself is a delightful word that comes from the Latin *scintilla,* meaning "a spark." In modern English a *scintilla* is "a spark," or "tiny particle," as in the phrase "not one scintilla." These glittering words are also related to English *tinsel.*

belong to a horsey set of words stemming from the Indo-European root **EKWO-,** meaning "horse." (Traces of this root are more clearly seen in Latin *equus,* the equivalent of Greek *hippos,* which now appears in English *equine* and *equestrian.*) **EKWO-**'s Greek descendant, *hippos,* is also part of the English word *hippodrome,* which originally referred to an ancient Greek racetrack, the name of which was formed by adding *hippos* to the Greek word *dromos,* which means "race," "running," or "racecourse." (More about this word's relatives, including *syndrome, palindrome,* and *dromedary,* in the chapter on **Daisy.**)

AMARYLLIS
. . .

The Greeks also added *hippos* to a term for "sea monster," *kampos,* to form the name of the mythical beast *Hippokampos,* which had the head of a horse and the tail of a fish. The Latin version of this word, *Hippocampus,* now serves as the name of the scientific genus to which the seahorses belong. In addition, the modern medical term *hippocampus* denotes each of two ridges inside the human brain—ridges that, when viewed from a certain angle, do look something like seahorses.

Greek *hippos* also rears its head in the name *Philip,* or "horse-loving," from Greek *philos,* which means "loving" or "friend." (A *philippic,* on the other hand, is hardly "loving." This word means "a bitter verbal attack" and commemorates the impassioned diatribes against King Philip II of Macedonia by the Greek orator Demosthenes.) To their word

5

for "horse" the Greeks also added *potamos,* or "river," to form the name of the riparian beast now called a *hippopotamus.* The *potamos* in this word also resides in the word *Mesopotamia,* the "fertile crescent" that lies in the middle—or in Greek, *mesos*—of the Tigris and Euphrates rivers.

The word *hippopotamus,* or "river-horse," by the way, illustrates the natural human tendency to apply the names of well-known animals to those that are less familiar. The word *porpoise,* for example, literally means "pig-fish," and is the result of crossing the Latin words *porcus,* "pig," and *piscis,* "fish" (as in the astrological sign *Pisces*). A similar idea inspired the German and French words for "porpoise," *Meerschwein* and *marsouin,* both of which literally translate as "marine swine." *Meerkats,* those cuddly, communal animals that often resemble prairie dogs standing on their hind legs, take their name from the Dutch word for "sea cat," an apparent allusion to the fact that they were brought to Europe "from overseas." Speakers of English have also bequeathed a barnyard-full of animal names to various ocean creatures, including *sea cow, sea calf, seahorse,* and *sea hog*—the last of which is, appropriately enough, another name for the porpoise.

AMARYLLIS, by the way, isn't the only familiar English word that is borrowed from the name of a shepherd in a Latin poem. Another such shepherd was the protagonist in a lengthy poem published in 1530 by a gifted Italian physician, Girolamo Fracastoro. At the time a plague widely known as *Morbus Gallicus,* or "the French disease," was sweeping through Europe. Dr. Fracastoro's poem tells the story of a fictitious shepherd who ignored his duty to worship Apollo and instead swore allegiance to an earthly king. Divine retribution followed swiftly, and the wayward shepherd fell victim to a dreadful disease. The shepherd's name was *Syphilus,* and as the doctor's poem explains:

AMARYLLIS

. . .

> . . . he who wrought this outrage was the first
> To feel his body ache, when sore accursed.
> And for his ulcers and their torturing,
> No longer would a tossing, hard couch bring
> Him sleep. With joints apart and flesh erased,
> Thus was the shepherd flailed and thus debased.
> And after him this malady we call
> *Syphilis.*

In the end the unfortunate shepherd is cured with an extract from the tropical guaiacum tree—a treatment that in real life was showing signs of success. Dr. Fracastoro's ingenious strategy for disseminating scientific information proved effective. Within a century the story of poor Syphilus became so popular that a form of his name had replaced *morbus gallicus* as the term for this disease.

Dr. Fracastoro's poem, composed entirely in good Latin hexameter, was highly regarded by the literati

7

of Renaissance Italy. The good doctor himself was also the subject of some bizarre stories. It was said he was born with a mouth so tiny that it had to be surgically enlarged with a razor. According to another tale, while holding her infant son in her arms, his mother was struck dead by a bolt of lightning, but young Girolamo miraculously survived.

To return to the more wholesome shepherd, Amaryllis, it's worth noting that the flower named in her honor sometimes goes by the name *belladonna lily,* the *belladonna* coming from the Italian for "beautiful lady." As so often happens with common flower names, however, the name *belladonna* also applies to an entirely different plant. The distinction between these two plants is extremely important, since the other *belladonna* is the poisonous plant also known as *deadly nightshade.*

The toxic *belladonna* plant is a source of atropine, an antispasmodic drug that was carried as a nerve-gas antidote by United States troops in the Persian Gulf war. Atropine is also commonly used by doctors to dilate the pupils for eye exams, and it was this property that inspired the name *belladonna.* It seems it once was fashionable for Italian women to put a few drops of atropine in their eyes, as an artificial means of making them more dazzling, more sparkling, more scintillating—like the natural beauty of a shepherd named Amaryllis.

Anthurium

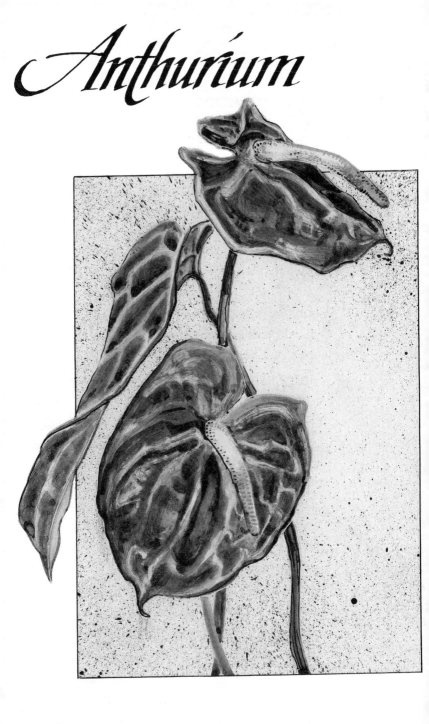

*T*he *anthurium* is easy to recognize by its long appendage drooping from a brilliant, heart-shaped leaf. This distinctive spadix inspired the flower's name, which combines the Latin stems *anth-*, or "flower," and *-urium,* "tail."

The *anth-* in the name of the anthurium originates from the Indo-European root called **ANDH-,** which means "to bloom." This root also gave rise to the Greek word for "flower," *anthos,* the source of such floral words in English as *anther,* "the pollen-bearing part of a blossom," and *anthesis,* "the period of a flower's full bloom." *Anth-* is part of such flower names as *chrysanthemum,* from Greek *khrusos,* "gold," and also seems to have influenced the name of the flower called *amaranth,* from Greek *amarantos,* "unwithering," "unfading."

Anthos is part of the Greek verb *exanthein,* "to bloom out," "burst forth," and thus in the medical term *exanthema,* a glorified word for "skin rash." The Greek word for "flower" also gave us one of the loveliest of English words, *anthology,* which literally means a "gathering of flowers," or "garland"—a literary bouquet, if you will.[1]

. . . .

[1] While it would be tempting to assume that Greek *anthos* is also in English *anthem,* this is not the case. *Anthem* is

SCHOLARS have followed the "tail," or -*urium,* in *anthurium* all the way back to the Indo-European root **ORS-,** which also means "tail." **ORS-** led to words for "tail" or "the fundament" in several languages, including German *Arsch,* Armenian *or,* and Old Irish *err,* as well as British *arse* and its American cousin, *ass.* (This *ass,* however, is different from the one that means "donkey." The latter type of "ass" apparently comes from some ancient language of Asia Minor, and is kin to such English words as *asinine* and *easel,* the wooden "beast of burden" that supports an artist's canvas.)

The prehistoric **ORS-** is also fossilized within the ancient Greeks' word for "tail," *oura,* which deserves a closer look, because it has some fascinating derivatives. The Greeks added *oura* to their word *skia,* or "shadow," to form the name of the animal they called "the shadow-tailed one," or *skiouros*— the forerunner of English *squirrel,* and *sciurine,* "of or pertaining to squirrels."[2]

The Greek word *skia,* by the way, is also in the name of the *Sciapodes,* or "shadow-footed ones," a

. . . .

adapted from the Medieval Latin word for a type of liturgical singing, *antiphona,* or "sung responses," from Greek *anti* and *phōnē,* "voice."

[2] The Germans, however, may have the most picturesque name for this animal: In German, a squirrel sometimes goes by the name *Eichkätzchen,* literally, "oak-kitten."

ANTHURIUM
. . .

legendary tribe thought to live in the hottest part of Libya. The Sciapodes, according to Greek myth, had such enormous feet that when the heat became too intense, they propped them up to use as sunshades. Aristophanes mentioned them in *The Birds:*

> 'Twas on that enchanted ground
> Where the Shadow-feet are found . . .

(Another ancient playwright, Euripides, used the word *skia* in a famous and typically Greek observation, *anthrōpos esti pneuma kai skia monon,* or "A human being is but a breath and a shadow.")

Greek *skia* has a few other shady English relatives, although they don't get out much. The word *sciagraph,* or literally, "shadow-writing," once meant "silhouette" and was briefly used as a synonym for "X-ray photograph." *Sciamachy,* from Greek *machē,* "battle" or "fight," is a glorified English term for "shadow-boxing."

BACK to tails and the *-urium* in *anthurium.* The Greeks also tacked their *oura* onto a form of their word for "dog," *kunos.* The result was *kunosoura,* or "dog's tail," a name the Greeks applied to the "handle" of the constellation now called the Little Dipper or Ursa Minor. The bright star at the end of this "handle" or "tail" is Polaris, the North Star, which for millennia served as a navigator's guide. From this sense of *kunosoura* as a "guiding star" came the English word *cynosure,* originally "a reference point or guide," and now "a center of attention."

ANTHURIUM

· · ·

While we're here, it's worth noting that Greek *kunos* arose from Indo-European **KWON-,** meaning "dog," a root that brought forth a large litter of interesting words. **KWON-** bounded into Latin as *canis,* or "dog," which is now part of English *canine, kennel,* and *canaille* (a "mob" or "rabble," but in the original French, "a pack of dogs"). Latin *canis* is also in the *Canary Islands,* named for the large dogs found roaming on them. It was only later that the yellow songbirds native to these islands inherited the same name.

Canis is also part of the name of another constellation, *Canis Major,* or "the larger dog." Within this constellation shines Sirius, the star which the Romans believed once had been the favorite hunting dog of Orion. They affectionately dubbed this star *Canicula,* or "little dog," and called the period in late summer when it rises and sets with the sun the *dies caniculares.* English-speaking folk borrowed and translated this phrase to denote the sweltering period now known as the *dog days.*

It's hard to resist a few other canine words before returning to the anthurium's "tail." The term for a painful inflammation of the tonsils, *quinsy,* comes from the Greeks' picturesque name for this malady, *kunanchē,* literally, "dog-strangle." *Kunokephaloi,* or "Dog-heads," was the ancient Greeks' name for a tribe in India whose members supposedly had

human bodies and dogs' heads. The historian Diodorus Siculus reported that these *Cynocephali,* as they are called in English, resembled "human beings of deformed visage" and were observed "sending forth human mutterings." Modern historians now suspect that such stories of a dog-headed race stemmed from travelers' sightings of apes or baboons.

If you doubt such tales, you may be called *cynical,* which is yet another "doggy" word. The sect of philosophers called the *Cynics* was founded by a student of Socrates. Just how this school of philosophy became associated with dogs is unclear. Some say it's because the Cynics regularly gathered in a gymnasium near Athens called the *Kunosarges,* a place supposedly named after a white dog. (More about the Greek word *argos,* or "white," in the chapter on **Hydrangea.**) It may be, however, that the name of the Cynics was inspired by their "snarling" or "currish" behavior, because the most dedicated Cynics scorned comfort, ate raw meat, neglected hygiene, and dispensed with common courtesy. Their most famous member, Diogenes, reportedly lived in a tub. Another, Peregrinus Proteus, is remembered chiefly for committing suicide by diving into the flames at the Olympic Games of 165 A.D.

To return again to anthuriums and tails: Perhaps you have at some time hesitated to send these provocative plants because their tails resemble an entirely different body part. If you thought so, you weren't off the mark, etymologically speaking. Among the many names the ancient Romans bestowed upon male genitalia was the Latin word *penis,* which means "tail." Apparently a similar notion inspired the dual meaning of a German word for "tail," *Schwanz,* which is also used as slang for "penis."

ANTHURIUM
. . .

A little Latin *penis* or "tail" is embedded in the English word *pencil,* which descended from a diminutive form of this word, *penicillus,* meaning "paintbrush," or literally, "a little tail." Similarly, the English word *pencil* first meant "paintbrush"—as in this 1591 text cited by the *Oxford English Dictionary,* or *OED:* "All the Chineans, Iaponians, and Cauchin Chineans do write right downwards, and they do write with a fine pensill made of dogs or cats haire." (The same idea is preserved in German, where the word *Pinsel* means "paintbrush," and the graphite writing instrument is called a *Bleistift.*) Likewise, the *penicillium* mold, which produces the antibiotic *penicillin,* also takes its name from Latin *penis,* because of the brushlike filaments that support its tiny spores.

Perhaps deciding not to send anthuriums might be considered *cowardly*—which, come to think of it, is yet another "tail" word. *Cowardly* comes from the Latin word *cauda,* which means "tail," as in the English word *caudate,* or "tailed." Scholars disagree about the exact progression from *cauda* to *cowardly:*

15

Some think that the English words *coward* and *cowardly* had their origins in the image of a rabbit bounding away in fright, or a spooked animal with its tail between its legs. Others speculate that these words allude to the sight of a cowardly soldier dashing to the "rear" of an army unit.

Latin *cauda* also produced several words that have been borrowed into English from other languages. Italian *coda,* or "tail," is a loanword that designates the end of a piece of music. Spanish *coleta,* or "little tail," now resides in English as the word for "the pigtail worn by a bullfighter." *Coleta* is the diminutive of Spanish *cola,* or "tail," which occasionally is used in English to mean "line" or "queue." In fact, the French loanword *queue* is another descendant of *cauda,* and is now used in English to mean either "a long line of people" or "a plait of hair"—a "pig-" or "pony-tail," in other words. French *queue* also started hanging out in pool halls, where it came to mean the long, tapering stick now spelled *c-u-e.* (This *cue,* however, is entirely different from an actor's *cue.* The *cue* that serves as a "hint" or "prompt" is of uncertain origin, although seventeenth-century writers insisted this word arose from the actors' practice of marking their parts in a script with the letter *q,* short for Latin *quando,* "when." No such annotated scripts have been discovered, but this explanation still makes more sense than any other that's been offered.) *Quando* is also found in the wise Latin proverb, *Quando plus ascendit symia, tanto plus apparent sua posterioria*—which loosely translates as, "The higher an ape climbs, the more it reveals of its behind." And with that warning in mind, we'll take our cue to conclude this etymological excursion prompted by that flower with a tail, the anthurium.

ANTHURIUM
. . .

Aster

*F*eeling starry-eyed? Then consider sending *asters* to the object of your desire. The root for *aster* shines through many words in several languages. The aster gets its name from an ancient Greek word for "star," *astēr.* Both Greek *astēr* and its English descendant derive from the Indo-European root **STER-3,** which means "star."

The ancient Greeks added *astēr* to their word for "appearance" or "form," *eidos,* to form *asteroeidēs,* their name for the "starlike" or "bright-shining" celestial bodies known to speakers of English as *asteroids.* The English word *asteroid,* by the way, also can be used as a synonym for "starfish."

The diminutive of Greek *astēr* was *asterikos,* which in turn led to the English word for a "little star," *asterisk.* The Greek verb *asterizein,* "to arrange in constellations," produced the term for the ghostly star that shimmers inside a sapphire, an *asterism.* The Greeks' word for "star" is also thought to have inspired their word for "lightning," *astrapē,* from which comes the English term for a morbid fear of lightning, *astraphobia.*

Speaking of morbid fears, Greek *aster* also shines inside *disaster,* an event that is "ill-starred." Centuries ago it was commonly believed that the stars influenced earthly events, and the word *disaster* referred in a most literal sense to "the evil influence of a star" or "an ominous sign in the heavens," as in this passage from *Hamlet:*

> In the most high and palmy state of Rome,
> A little ere the mightiest Julius fell,
> The graves stood tenantless, and the sheeted dead
> Did squeak and gibber in the Roman streets;
> As stars with trains of fire, and dews of blood,
> Disasters in the sun; and the moist star
> Upon whose influence Neptune's empire stands
> Was sick almost to doomsday with eclipse.

(The "moist star" mentioned here, by the way, is the moon.)

THE ancient Greeks were well acquainted with long-haired stars, though not the sort that today make astronomical amounts of money by singing or lip-synching. The Greek expression *astēr komētēs*— or literally, "long-haired star"—denoted a celestial phenomenon, the name of which was later shortened into the English word for that "star with long tresses," a *comet*.

Greek *astēr* also shines within the name of the star-sailors who travel in spaceships, the *astronauts.* The *naut* in their name is from the Indo-European root **NĀU-2,** meaning "boat," a root that launched a whole fleet of *nautical* words. In Latin, **NĀU-2** produced *navis,* or "ship," which in turn led to English *navy* and *navigate.* The Greek counterpart of Latin *navis* was *naus,* and a "sailor" who traveled in a *naus* was called a *nautēs,* or in poetic language, a *nautilos.* The Greeks also used the name *nautilos* for a spiral-shelled marine animal that was believed to use its ribbed arms like tiny sails—the creature now known in English as the *nautilus.* Any ancient Greek *nautilos* who endured a particularly rocky ride on the high seas was likely to experience the "ship-sickness" called *nausia,* the forerunner of English *nausea.* Some etymologists think that this queasy term also led to an Old French word meaning "outcry" or "loud dispute," which later found its way into English as the word *noise.*

ASTER

. . .

THE "starry" Indo-European root **STER-3** also gave rise to the Latin word for "star," *stella,* the source of the words for "star" in several other languages, including Spanish *estrella,* Portuguese *estrela,* Italian *stella,* French *étoile,* and Romanian *stea.* In English, Latin *stella* is also responsible for a whole *constellation* of words, including *stellar, interstellar, stelliform* (which describes a starfish or anything else "star-shaped"), *stellify* ("to make into a star"), and the old song "Stella by Starlight."

One of Latin *stella*'s most fascinating English derivatives is *stellionate,* a legal term denoting a kind of fraud, especially the sort perpetrated when someone sells something that doesn't belong to him or her—the Brooklyn Bridge, for example—or sells the same property to more than one buyer. The term *stellionate* derives from the Latin word *stellio,* which the Romans applied to a type of lizard that had stelliform markings on its back. This particular lizard was supposedly quite crafty, and eventually the Romans applied its name to any person who showed similar cunning. Thus also the Latin term *stellionatus* came to mean "trickery" or "cheating."

Stellio darted into English as a synonym for "lizard." In fact, the word *stellio* was once such a common English word that it was used in Miles Coverdale's 1535 translation of the Bible, which renders Leviticus 11:30 as, "These shal be vncleane . . . the Hedgehogge, the Stellio . . ." (The Coverdale Bible, incidentally, is also known as the "Bug Bible," because it translates Psalms 91:5 as "Thou shalt not nede to be afrayed for eny *bugges* by night." Other versions use the word *terror.* The word *bug* itself, interestingly enough, is germane to a discussion of the English word *aster* and its stellar relatives: In racetrack parlance, the weight allowance for apprentice jockeys is called a *bug,* a term inspired by the punctuation mark that designates this allowance on a racing form—*bug* being printers' slang for "asterisk.")

HAVING considered derivatives of **STER-3** in the languages of ancient Greece and Rome, we should note that **STER-3** is also represented in the language of the ancient Persians, where it became *sitareh,* or "star." This Persian word also led to the Hebrew name *'Estēr* and its English counterpart *Esther.* Many scholars link the ancient Hebrew name *'Estēr* with that of the Babylonian goddess Ishtar, citing, among other things, the similarities between the Hebrew scriptures' story of the Jewish queen Esther and her uncle Mordecai, and that of the Babylonian cousins Ishtar and Marduk.

ASTER

. . .

VIA the Germanic language branch of Indo-European languages, the root **STER-3** found its way into the English word *star. Star* appears in a host of heavenly expressions, one of the most intriguing of which is *star jelly,* a blue-green algae held together by a strange kind of gelatinous goo. Star jelly is so named because it spreads with such speed overnight that it was once thought to have fallen from the stars. This curious substance earned several other evocative names as well, including *star-slime* and *witches' butter* in English, as well as Swedish *trollsmör,* "troll's butter." [1]

STER-3 also produced the German word for "star," *Stern.* In the German language, as in English,

. . . .

[1] It may be that a trace of English *star* also glimmers within the name of the standard British currency called *sterling,* because medieval pennies were stamped with a star. However, some scholars maintain that this word's etymology remains unclear.

an asterisk is a "little star," or *Sternchen*. The word *Stern* is also found in some lively German compounds, such as *Sterngucker*, or "stargazer" (from *gucken*, "to look," "peep at"). *Stern* is also part of one of the Germans' many vivid words involving intoxication, *sternhagelvoll*, which means "extremely drunk." Literally this term translates as "star-hail-full"—"blitzed," in other words.

CONTRARY to appearances, the English word *poet-aster* does not indicate a stellar poet, and a *philoso-phaster* is hardly a star philosopher. The English word *aster* and all its astral kin are unrelated to *-aster*, which was borrowed from Latin as a suffix indicating something "small," "inferior," or "less than it pretends to be." An equivalent of this suffix appears more frequently in the Romance languages, especially French, where *bleuâtre* means "bluish" and *blanchâtre*, "whitish." The Latin suffix *-aster* is, however, represented in a few English words, including *criticaster*, which *Webster's* defines as "an inferior or contemptible critic," and *politicaster*, which is one of those splendid old words that should have never fallen out of use, considering that it's such a handy means of saying "a poor excuse for a politician."

Another word that also masquerades as a linguistic relative of *aster* and *star* is the English term *star-board*, which refers to the "right-hand side of a ship." This term comes from Old English *stēorbord*, *stēor* being the "steering" oar or rudder, which was manipulated from the right side of a vessel. The *bord* in this case means "the side of a ship," and thus also appears in that other nautical term, *overboard.*

LOOK back to the second sentence of this chapter, and you may detect "stars" in two other words besides *asters.* That's because the words *consider* and *desire* both come from the Latin word *sidus,* yet another term for "star" or "constellation." Latin *sidus* arose from another Indo-European root meaning "to shine," **SWEID-1.**

In its earliest sense, the Latin verb *considerare* means "to observe the stars in order to predict the future." The Latin verb *desiderare,* formed by analogy with *considerare,* means "to investigate" or "long for." Thus Latin *sidus,* "star," still shines faintly inside English *consider* and *desire,* as well as in the four-syllable adjective *sidereal,* which means "pertaining to the stars," and the verb *siderate,* "to blast or strike down (as with lightning)."

Of course, the belief that the stars can influence earthly matters is hardly new. Even the word *influence* itself reflects this idea: It comes from Latin *influentia,* a "flowing-in," which is a form of Latin *fluere,* "to flow." (Latin *fluere* is also the source of *fluid, fluent,* and *affluence*—the last of these being caused by an *influx* of wealth). Once it was widely believed that *influence* was literally an ethereal fluid that "flowed in" to the earth from the stars and altered the course of human affairs. When, for example, an infectious fever raged through Italy in the mid-eighteenth century, the Italians referred to it by the same name they had long used for any epidemic caused by the stars' "evil influence." This particular outbreak, however, spread far beyond Italy—and so did its name, which in English became *influenza* or, in shortened form, *flu*.

Even in modern times, there are some who still consider it prudent to consult the stars before making decisions—or at least to pay an astrologer to do it for them. For example, it was revealed that astrologers played a key role in arranging former president Ronald Reagan's daily schedule in order to avoid possible disasters. Such revelations would lend a whole new meaning to accusations of "influence peddling," especially in an administration that was headed by a politician—or, some would say, a politicaster—who was once something of a star himself.

Chrysanthemum

*I*t should be relatively easy to pick out the *anth-,* or "flower," in the word *chrysanthemum.*[1] The *chrys-* in *chrysanthemum* comes from the Greek word for "gold," *khrusos,* which was probably adapted in turn from a word in a Semitic language. The ancient Greeks used the name *khrusanthemon* to denote several types of gold-colored blossoms. Today, however, the Latinized scientific name *Chrysanthemum* designates a genus of popular, fall-blooming flowers that are not only yellow, but come in a wide range of colors, from white to dark red.

The Greek *khrusos* in *chrysanthemum* is also part of the rather elephantine English word *chryselephantine.* This term, which means "made of gold and ivory," describes some of the finest artwork in antiquity. The latter part of this word comes from Greek *elephas,* which could mean either "elephant" or "ivory," and preceded the English word *elephant.* The famous statuettes of Cretan snake goddesses with their arms upraised are *chryselephantine,* as were the colossal statues that stood inside major

. . . .

[1] Especially if you have read about *anth-* and its other floral offspring in the chapter on **Anthurium.**

Greek temples, including the forty-foot-tall likeness of Athena in the Parthenon—the building that honors Athena *Parthenos,* or "Athena the Virgin," as in *parthenogenesis,* or "virgin birth."

CHRYSANTHEMUM

· · ·

The Greek word for "gold" is also part of the name of *St. John Chrysostom,* one of the early patriarchs of the Christian church. Famed for his enthusiastic persecution of pagans and his zealous preaching against worldly pleasures—he himself spent six years living in a cave—Chrysostom was also renowned for his eloquence, and hence received his name, which means "golden mouth." (Greek *stoma,* or "mouth," by the way, also inspired the word for the pouch at the end of one's gullet, the *stomach.*)

Chrysoprase is a gem named for its "gold and bright green" tint. The *-prase* in its name comes from the Greeks' word for "leek," *prason.* Chrysoprase, in the biblical book of Revelation, is among the twelve glittering foundations of the pearly-gated city of Jerusalem. (This must have been splendid indeed, since these layers included sapphire, emerald, amethyst, and *chrysolite,* or literally, "gold-stone.") In the Middle Ages, people believed that *chrysoprase* could shine in the dark and that by tucking it under the tongue one could become invisible. Another gem, *chrysoberyl,* or "gold-beryl," really is magical: In natural sunlight this gem is brilliant grass-green, but under artificial light it turns red. Chrysoberyl is

also known as *alexandrite,* having been discovered in the Ural Mountains and named after a Russian czar.[2]

Certain insect larvae work some real-life magic of their own by spinning themselves a hard, cocoonlike shell called a *chrysalis.* Inside this structure, the larva's body dissolves and rearranges itself into a magnificent winged insect. The Greek word *khrusallis* refers to "the gold-colored sheath" of certain butterflies. The chrysalis of the monarch butterfly, by the way, is a stunning combination of glistening aquamarine and what looks exactly like drops of liquid gold.

THE Italian equivalent of *chrysalis* is *aurelia,* a word also adopted into English as a synonym for "chrysalis." The word *aurelia* comes from Latin *aurum,* meaning "gold," another word that is not, strictly speaking, of Indo-European origin. Latin *aurum,* however, can be mined from several modern English terms, including *aureole,* or "halo," *oriole* (which is

. . . .

[2] The *beryl,* or "precious stone," in the name *chrysoberyl* has a fascinating history as well. Its Greek ancestor, *bērullos,* was most likely borrowed from some Eastern source. Its Medieval Latin derivative, *berillus,* came to be used as a synonym for "crystal," and in sixteenth-century England various spellings of the term *beryl-glass* were used for "mirror." This sense also led to the use of modern French *besicles* and German *Brille* for "eyeglasses." *Beryl* may also be kin to the English word *brilliant.*

discussed at greater length in the chapter on **Columbine**), and the chemical symbol for "gold," *Au.*

CHRYSANTHEMUM

· · ·

Latin *aurum* is part of the Medieval Latin *auriflamma,* or "gold flame," which produced *oriflamme,* the name of the red-orange flag that served as the symbol of French royalty until it was replaced by the *fleur-de-lis.* In English the word *oriflamme* is now extended to mean "any inspiring flag or symbol." From this family of words also comes the Latin word *auripigmentum,* or "gold pigment." By a logical concatenation of events, *auripigmentum* became English *orpiment,* the name of a brilliant yellow, arsenic-based pigment—and in turn gave rise to the name of another flower, *orpine.* The hardy orpine also goes by the name *live-forever,* because it seems to.[3]

Finally, take a moment to look at the picturesque word *concatenation* in that last paragraph. This word comes from the Latin stem *com-,* meaning "together," and *catena,* "chain." Latin *catena* is related to such words as English *chain* and Spanish *cadena.* The ancient Latin writer Pliny the Elder appears to have used the word *catena* specifically to designate "a chain of gold"—which, come to think of it, is what we've been following from word to word to word, starting with the name of that golden flower, the *chrysanthemum.*

· · · · · · · · · · · · · · · · · · · ·

[3] Actually the flower now called orpine has purplish-red blossoms; its name is thought to be inspired by the yellow flowers of a related species.

Columbine

*A*s an adjective, the English word *columbine* describes anything that is "dovelike." So it is that the *columbine* flower was named for the way the horned tips of its blossoms resemble a cluster of little doves, all turturring to one another.

Both the adjective *columbine* and the name of this elegant flower derive from the Latin word *columba,* which means "dove." From the same source comes the English word *columbary,* or "dovecote." A person's cremated remains are sometimes stored in a *columbarium,* a type of funerary vault that looks something like a dovecote, with its rows of niches for urns containing ashes.

The dove, of course, has been identified with divinity ever since prehistoric times when it was used to signify various goddesses worshipped in Asia Minor. In early Christian art, the columbine's uncanny resemblance to a huddle of doves also made this flower an apt symbol for the Holy Spirit. By the late Middle Ages, however, church-commissioned artists stopped using this flower in their work, apparently because the columbine had acquired another meaning—as a symbol of the cuckold, a husband whose wife commits adultery. At that time cuckoldry was increasingly

associated with the cuckoo, a bird notorious for laying its eggs in other birds' nests. The allusion was a familiar one to Shakespeare's audiences, and thus at the end of *Love's Labor's Lost* the Bard wrote:

> The cuckoo then on every tree
> Mocks married men; for thus sings he,
>   "Cuckoo;
> Cuckoo, Cuckoo"—O word of fear,
> Unpleasing to a married ear.

Many historians surmise that the columbine flower fell out of favor with the Church as people realized the columbine might just as readily resemble cuckoos as doves.

Speaking of romance, the word *Columbine* is immortalized also as the name of a stock character in Italian comedy, the "dovelike" but spirited young woman who had an on-again-off-again love affair with the fellow in the diamond-patterned tights, Harlequin.

THE name *columbine* and its linguistic ancestor, Latin *columba*, "dove," stem from the Indo-European root called **KEL-5**, which connotes the idea of "gray," "dark," or "black." Latin *columba* apparently developed from the notion of the "dusky color" of doves and pigeons.[1] Although **KEL-5** is responsible for only a handful of words in English, it produced some fascinating descendants in Russian, where *golub'* means "dove," *goluboy* means "pale blue," *goluboglazyy* means "blue-eyed," and *golubit'* is a wonderfully vivid means of saying "to caress or fondle (as doves do)." This last idea is also reflected in the Latin verb *columbari,* "to bill or kiss like doves."

COLUMBINE

· · ·

The English word *dove* itself is the product of another Indo-European root that means "dark" or "dusky," **DHEU-1,** which seems to have led to a variety of words related to the ideas of "dark color," "smoke," "dust," and by extension, "defective perception." These linguistic relatives of English *dove* include *dusk, dust,* and *dun* (the color—not the sending of an invoice). This same dark and dusty root led to the words *fume, obfuscate,* and *deaf,* the last of these connoting the idea of "clouded perception."

WORDS such as English *dove* and Latin *columba* are among the many examples of a widespread tendency to create names for animals based on their color.

· · · · · · · · · · · · · · · · · · ·

[1] The *columbine* flower is also called *culverwort.* English *culver,* or "dove," may be yet another descendant of Latin *columba,* although this remains a matter of scholarly dispute.

Another such "bird word," for example, is Latin *palumbes,* meaning "pigeon" or "ring dove." *Palumbes* comes from the Indo-European root **PEL-2,** which means "pale," and is the source of English *pale, pallor, pallid,* and *appalling* (which describes something that causes one to "grow pale"). **PEL-2** also produced the Greek word for "gray," *polios,* which in turn colors the English word *poliomyelitis,* the inflammation of the spinal cord's "gray matter," better known as *polio.* The pallid color in **PEL-2** is also apparently reflected in the Germanic languages, including the English animal names *falcon,* a "gray bird," and *fallow,* which refers to the pale reddish-yellow color of a *fallow deer.*

PEL-2's Latin offspring, *palumbes,* or "dove," in turn gave rise to the Spanish word for "dove," *paloma.* (The diminutive of this word, *palomitas,* is sometimes used in Spanish as a synonym for "popcorn.") The pale Spanish *paloma* also inspired the name of a horse with a "dusky" or "dovelike" color, the *palomino.* This word's Italian cousin, *palombino,* or "dovelike," also emigrated into English, where it means a type of "light-gray marble."

This link between the names of animals and their coloration occurs with striking frequency, often with surprising results. The rest of this chapter examines several instances of this phenomenon in a variety of languages.

· · ·

THE names of many other gray animals were inspired by their color. The Latvian word for "mouse," *pele,* literally means "gray," and is yet another of those pale words that skittered out of Indo-European **PEL-2.** Another Indo-European root, **GHER-3,** which means "to shine" or "glow," produced several "gray" words, including English *greyhound* and *grayling,* the latter of which applies to both a type of gray fish and several varieties of grayish butterflies. **GHER-3** also shines through the name of the *grizzly bear,* which was inspired by its "gray" or *grizzled* fur, and through *grison,* a small gray mammal of Central and South America. Other offspring of **GHER-3** include Old Norse *gríss,* or "pig," and a French synonym for "squirrel," *petit-gris,* "the little gray one." The addition of French *gris,* "gray," to *vert,* or "green," produced the name of the *grivet,* a close relative of the animal known to English speakers as the *green monkey.*

Yet another Indo-European root meaning "gray," **KAS-,** produced the name of the gray animal known in English as a *hare* and its cognates, including German *Hase,* Welsh *ceinach,* and Sanskrit *śaśas.* (Incidentally, such a correspondence of the initial letters *h, c,* and *s* is not as unlikely as it might seem. Consider the offspring of Indo-European **KWON-,** "dog," which include German *Hund* and English *hound,* Latin *canis* and English *canine,* and a Sanskrit word for "dog," *śvās.* Similarly **KER-1,** or "horn,"

COLUMBINE

. . .

led to German *Horn,* English *horn,* Latin *cornu*—as in *cornet* and *cornucopia,* "horn of plenty"—and in Sanskrit, *śṛṅga,* "horn.") **KAS-** is also part of the lovely English word *canescent,* which means "becoming white or grayish," as in "the canescent moon."

AMONG the animal names referring to "white" is the Russian word for "swan," *lebed',* which was formed by metathesis from a Latin word for "white," *albus.*[2] Latin *albus* is also the source of such words as *albino, Albion* (a name that may refer to the "white cliffs" of Dover), and the delightful word *aubade,* "a song sung at dawn or 'first light.' " Some scholars think that Latin *albus* may also have influenced the name of the white seabird called an *albatross.* The exact etymology of this word remains unclear, but it may be that English-speaking sailors confused the name with that of another large seafowl which Spaniards called an *alcatraz.*

The Russian word for "white," *belyy* (as in *byelorussian,* or "White Russian"), is responsible for *beluga,* a type of sturgeon that is the source of *beluga caviar.* The name *beluga* is also applied to a "white whale" of the northern seas. *Beluga* and *belyy* come

• •

[2] *Metathesis* is the transposition of letters, sounds, or syllables that sometimes occurs in the development of a word. English *bird,* for example, arose from an Old English word, *brid.*

from the Indo-European root **BHEL-1,** meaning "bright," "shining," or "shining white." This root also appears in the Greek word *phalaros,* "marked with a patch of white," which inspired the name of the bird called a *phalarope,* which has a spot of white on its head. The same idea led to the name of the *blesbok,* an African antelope with a white mark on its head, whose name comes from Middle Dutch *bles* (yet another product of **BHEL-1**) and *bok,* meaning "buck."

COLUMBINE
· · ·

Similarly, some scholars trace the name *penguin* to the Welsh *pen gwyn,* or "white head"—a reference to the distinctive dab of white near the eyes in certain species of penguins. (Other authorities suggest that the "white head" in the penguin's name refers instead to a white promontory on an isle near Newfoundland, where these birds were found in abundance in the 1500s. Still others insist that this word's origin remains unclear.) Welsh *gwyn,* at any rate, is kin to the Scottish Gaelic word *fionn,* which also means "white" and is the source of the name of a pale sea trout called *finnock,* as well as the name *Fiona.*

One last animal named for its whiteness is the *opossum,* whose name derives from an Algonquian word, spelled either *âpäsûm* or *aposoum,* meaning "the white animal." In Cherokee tradition the first opossum was completely white, but longed to have a brown tail and tried to get one by toasting his tail over a fire. Of course the scheme backfired, so to

speak, and now every opossum is white with a bare tail.

MANY animals that are dark or black have names describing them as such. The *siamang* is a monkey with long black hair whose name comes from the Malay *āmang,* or "black." The cat known as a *caracal* takes its name from Turkish *karakulak,* literally, "black ear."

The fish called *perch* was known to the Greeks as *perkē,* a name thought to be related to the Greek adjective *perknos,* meaning "dark," "dusky." Another fish, the *mullet,* derives its name from an Indo-European root meaning "dark," **MEL-2,** also the source of the "dark" words *melanin* and *melancholy.*[3]

From Indo-European **BHER-3,** a root meaning "brown" or "bright," come the English words *bear, bruin,* and *beaver,* as well as *Bern,* the Swiss capital which takes its name from German *Bären,* "bears," and features a bear on its coat of arms. **BHER-3** is also found in the ancient Greek word *phrunē,* or

. . . .

[3] This root also apparently produced English *mule,* meaning "a shoe or slipper lacking a strap around the heel." This type of mule is the offspring of the Latin word *mulleus,* which denotes the deep-red or purple shoes worn by top Roman magistrates. (*Mule* as in "donkey" stems from a non–Indo-European source and thus its origins are obscure.)

"toad." This animal's Greek name is now part of the English medical term *phrynoderma,* a rough, dry skin eruption, as well as *phrynin,* a poison secreted in the glands of certain toads. **BHER-3,** by the way, also produced the English words *brown, brunet,* and *burnish.*

COLUMBINE

. . .

SOME of the more colorful words associated with animals include the name of the bright-yellow European bird called an *oriole,* whose name derives ultimately from Latin *aurum,* "gold." Later the name *oriole* was also applied to the black and orange bird whose plumage calls to mind the colors on the coat of arms belonging to the family of English colonists in Maryland known as the *Baltimores.*

Latin *aurum,* "gold," also inspired the name of a fish with a metallic yellow sheen, the *dory,* via the French word *dorée,* or "gilded." The same Latin word shines through Spanish *dorado,* the name of a colorful fish, as in *El Dorado,* or "The Gilded Land," the legendary paradise sought by sixteenth-century Spanish conquistadors.

The bird called a *cardinal* is named for its bright red feathers, which recall the brilliant crimson robes worn by Catholic church officials of the same name. Latin *cardo* means "hinge," and the *cardinals* of the Catholic church are so named because the hierarchy's administration "hinges" upon them. Thus also the English adjective *cardinal* means, in its most literal sense, "pivotal," as in "a cardinal event." An-

other animal named for its red color is the *rorqual,* a whale whose name derives from Old Norse *reythar-hvalr,* literally, "red whale"—a reference to its red streaks.

You'd think that the orange ape called an *orang-utan* would be yet another of these animals named for their color, but it's not. In the picturesque Malay language, *ōrang* means "person" and *hūtan* means forest; thus this animal is simply a "forest dweller." (According to writer James Fallows, the word *ōrang,* along with the Malay word for "broken," *cacat,* can be found posted on signs in some Malaysian bathrooms, indicating that the restroom is accessible to the disabled.)

SOMETIMES the psychological connection between animals and colors works in the opposite direction, so that the word for a particular color is borrowed from an animal's name. That perennial pantyhose color *taupe,* for example, is a borrowing of a French word with the same spelling. French *taupe* refers to the burrowing animal known to English speakers as a "mole." *Taupe* comes from the Latin word for "mole," *talpa.* Latin *talpa* is also burrowed inside the Italian word for "mouse" or "rat," *topo,* which should be familiar to anyone old enough to remember Ed Sullivan's sometime sidekick, *Topo Gigio.*

Finally, the name of the color *puce* also arose from that of a living creature, and in a most marvelous way. *Puce* comes from the Indo-European root

PLOU-, meaning "flea." Having hopped along the Germanic branch of Indo-European languages, this root eventually found its way to English as the word *flea*.

COLUMBINE
· · ·

The Latin word for "flea," *pulex,* also derives from this root, and remains with us today in the English word *pulicide,* or "flea-killer." Latin *pulex* gave rise to the word for "flea" in Spanish, *pulga,* and in French, *puce.* The French expression *couleur puce,* or "flea color," came about as a reference to the color of these blood-sucking pests, presumably their color after they have been squished. (John Donne's strange poem "The Flea" makes reference to someone "purpling" her nail by smashing a flea.) *Puce* was for a time a most fashionable color at the French court. The *OED* cites a 1776 publication in which a writer mentions a "new-fashioned flea-colored coat" and a 1794 work that refers to "a brilliant flea-brown color."

The Greek cousin of Latin *pulex* is *psulla,* which also means "flea." This word was borrowed whole into English as the name of a kind of plant lice, and as part of the word *psyllium,* the scientific term for a grain rich in water-soluble fiber. When moist, psyllium's tiny, "flealike" seeds become swollen and gelatinous, making them an effective ingredient in laxatives. In fact, some breakfast cereal companies now boast that their product contains psyllium, an ingredient that sounds wonderfully salubrious. No doubt some well-paid advertising executive wisely

43

chose to use this high-fiber grain's scientific name, rather than its more common name, *fleawort*.

While we're on the subject, a final word about fleas. The name of the musical instrument *ukulele* combines the Hawaiian word *'uku,* which means "flea" or "tiny person," and *lele,* which means "jumping." The ukulele is said to be named in honor of Edward Purvis, a British army officer credited with popularizing this instrument, which was first brought to the islands by Portuguese laborers. Purvis was famed for his strikingly small stature and nimble movements, as well as for his passionate love for the ukulele. The Hawaiians' nickname for this frenetic fellow became synonymous with the diminutive ukulele—which, as you may recall, is tuned to the musical mnemonic, "My dog has fleas."

Daisy

When evening brings the merry folding hours, and sun-eyed daisies close their winking flowers . . .

A s nineteenth-century poet John Leyden observed, some species of the *daisy* close their blossoms at night. For this reason, speakers of Old English called this flower a *daeges ēage,* or "day's eye." Eventually the name of this cheery little "eye of the day" was condensed into a single word, *daisy.*

The origin of *day, daisy,* and their Old English ancestor, *daeg,* is surprisingly difficult to trace. Some scholars think that these words, along with English *dawn,* arose from an Indo-European root designated as **AGH-2,** which denotes "the span of time covered by a day." However, this explanation leaves unanswered the question of just how the initial *d* sound came to be added to this root's descendants. Other scholars suspect that *day* is the linguistic offspring of a different Indo-European root, which they reconstruct as **DHEGH-,** "to burn." **DHEGH-,** according to these experts, may be the source of words in several languages indicating "a time when the sun is hot," such as Lithuanian *dāgas,* or "harvest time."

It's important to note here that quite a few words pertaining to "daytime" appear to be linguistically related to the word *day* but are not. Such words as *diary,* "a day's record," and Spanish *día,* "day," derive from the Latin word for "day," *dies,* which comes from still another Indo-European root, **DEIW-,** "to shine." In fact, this root produced so many fascinating offspring—including the word for "day" in several other languages—that it merits a closer look.

DAISY

· · ·

As noted above, **DEIW-** produced Latin *dies,* or "day," part of which now remains in the medical abbreviations *b.i.d.* and *t.i.d.,* for *bis in die,* "twice a day," and *ter in die,* "three times a day," now used when writing prescriptions. Latin *dies* also lingered a while in English within the obsolete but seemingly handy word *nudiustertian,* which means "pertaining to the day before yesterday." (*Nudiustertian* comes from Latin *nunc dies tertius est,* or literally, "now it is the third day.) A form of Latin *dies* is also in the expression *per diem,* or "per day," as well as in the Latin phrase *Carpe diem,* literally, "Seize the day!" —or in other words, "Grab the opportunity!" [1]

Dies also led to the Late Latin word *diurnum,*

· · · · · · · · · · · · · · · · · · · ·

[1] *Carpe,* by the way, belongs to a fascinating family of words deriving from Indo-European **KERP-,** "to gather," "pluck," "harvest." Its members include such words as English *harvest* and German *Herbst,* which means "autumn" or "harvest time," as well as *excerpt,* which is something "plucked from" a text, and *carpet,* which is "made by plucking" threads.

meaning "day," which in turn produced English *diurnal,* which means "occurring in daytime" or "daily." At one time, the word *diurnal* was also commonly used as an English synonym for "diary" or "daily newspaper." Latin *diurnum* also makes an appearance in the French word for "day," *jour,* as in *bon* and *soup du.* This French word for "day," in turn, found its way into English in *journal,* a "diary" or "day's record," *journey,* originally "a day's travel," and *adjourn,* "to put off until an appointed day."

In prehistoric times, a variant of **DEIW-,** "to shine," came to be associated with the ideas of "sky," "heaven," and "divinity." As a result, **DEIW-** is reflected in various names for the "god of the bright sky"—the deity whose name became *Zeus* in Greek, and *Jove* in Latin. (The name *Jupiter* literally means "Jove father," the *-piter* here being kin to such *paternal* words as English *father* and its counterparts, which include German *Vater,* Dutch *vader,* French *père,* and Spanish *padre.*)

The "shining" root **DEIW-** also led to the names of some northern European deities, including *Tiu,* the Germanic god of war and the sky—to whom speakers of English pay homage whenever they mention the day after Monday, which is named in his honor. This practice of naming the days of the week after gods is mirrored in several Romance languages, where *Tuesday* is named after the Roman god of war,

Mars. In Spanish this day is called *martes,* in Italian, *martedì,* and in French, *mardi,* as in *Mardi Gras,* or "Fat Tuesday."

DAISY

. . .

DEIW- also shines through two Latin words for "god." One of them, *divus,* is the source of English *divine* and *diva.* The other, *deus,* is found in English *deity,* as well as both French *adieu* and Spanish *adiós,* the farewells that literally commend someone "to God." Here let us seize the opportunity to adjourn this discussion of "day" words, bid adieu to these shining examples of **DEIW-**'s descendants, and journey on into the *eye* of the *daisy.*

IN contrast to the English word *day,* the *eye* inside the name of the daisy has a well-established etymological history. The word *eye* comes from another prolific Indo-European root, **OKW-,** meaning "to see," which produced a host of words involving the notions of "eye," "sight," or "appearance." **OKW-** is the source of the word for "eye" in several languages, including Spanish *ojo,* Italian *occhio,* Portuguese *olho,* Dutch *oog,* German *Auge,* Old Russian *óko,* and Sanskrit *ákshi.*

OKW- is visible in the ancient Greek words *ōps, optos, ophthalmos,* and *opsis,* all of which involve "the eye" or "appearance" and led to several significant English derivatives. When *ōps,* or "eye," was added to the Greek verb *muein,* "to shut," for example, the result was *muōpia,* and in English, *myopia*

49

—a word that makes perfect sense to anyone who must squint to see at a distance. (Greek *muein,* "to shut," is also tucked into the word *mystery,* which in its most literal sense reflects the "closed lips" or "secrecy" expected of those initiated into the ancient mystery cults.)

Greek *optos,* meaning "seen" or "visible," is now detectable in such English words as *optical* and *optometrist,* "one who measures vision." A related Greek word for "eye," *ophthalmos,* now peeks out of the English word *ophthalmology*—the troublesome spelling of which becomes easier if you bear in mind that the first *o* is followed by two Greek double consonants, *phi,* or ϕ, as in *Phi Beta Kappa,* and *theta,* which looks sort of like a *phi* that fell over: θ.

Another of **OKW-**'s Greek offspring, *opsis,* meaning "sight" and thus also "appearance" or "countenance," led to several English derivatives. Added to the preposition *sun,* or "with," *opsis* became *sunopsis,* the ancestor of English *synopsis*—a "viewing all together" or "summary," in other words. From Greek *autos,* "self," came the Greeks' word *autopsia,* the "seeing with one's own eyes" that is the predecessor of the English term for a postmortem examination, *autopsy.* (In contrast, the examination of living tissue is called a *biopsy,* a word that, like *biology,* comes from Greek *bios,* "life.")

When Greek *opsis,* or "appearance," was combined with the word for "bedbug," *koris,* the result was *coreopsis,* the flower named for its seeds, which

50

have tiny antennalike projections that make them resemble bugs. Not surprisingly, coreopsis also goes by the name *tickseed.* Sometimes gardeners and nursery owners try to improve upon this flower's unfortunate name by calling it *calliopsis,* or literally "beautiful appearance." (More about calliopsis and its lovely linguistic relatives in the chapter on **Lily.**)

DAISY
· · ·

The Greeks added their word *opsis,* in the sense of "face" or "countenance," to their word *aithein,* "to burn," to form the name of the Africans they called *Aithiops,* or the "burned-face" ones—a name preserved in modern English as *Ethiopian.* (In reality, the skin tone of the Ethiopians varied widely. The early ruling tribes of Ethiopia were in fact Semitic, and Arabs derisively referred to their land as *habesha,* or "mixed"—a name Westerners later corrupted to *Abyssinia.*[2]

A form of Greek *opsis,* "face," is also found in a celebrated Greek palindrome—a word or phrase that can be read backward or forward, such as *radar,*

· · · · · · · · · · · · · · · · · · · ·

[2] The Greeks' word *aithein,* or "burn," also produced their term for the "blazing-bright heavens," *aether,* which became English *ether.* Many etymologists think *aithein* also glows inside the name of Mount *Aetna,* the fiery volcano that housed the forge of Vulcan, blacksmith of the Roman gods. Vulcan's own namesakes include English *volcano* and *vulcanization,* the process of using intense heat to improve the strength and resiliency of rubber.

race car, *Madam, I'm Adam,* and *Nurse, so no noses
run.*[3] (Michael Gartner's newspaper column,
"Words, Words, Words," recently included the gem
Drat Saddam, mad dastard.) The Greek palindrome
that contains a form of *opsis* is *Nipson anomēmata
mē monan opsin.*[4] Inscribed on baptismal fonts in
parts of Greece and Turkey, this palindrome means
"Wash my transgressions, not just my face." As long
as we're on the subject of palindromes about absolv-
ing guilt—it's not every day, after all, that this topic
comes up—here's one in Latin, supposedly penned
by a Roman lawyer: *Si nummi immunis,* which translates into something like "Give me your fee and
you'll get off scot-free."

. . . .

[3] *Palindrome* literally means "a running back again." The
-*drome* in *palindrome* comes from Greek *dromos,* "running," also found in *hippodrome,* a "racecourse for
horses," and that speedy, one-humped runner of the desert, the *dromedary.* Similarly, by adding the Greek prefix
sun, or "with," to *dromos,* the Greeks came up with the
linguistic predecessor of English *syndrome*—literally a
"running together" or "combination" of symptoms. The
palin- in *palindrome* means "again," and is part of English
palinode, originally a poem in which the writer retracts an
assertion, and now a verbal retraction of any kind, especially a formal one.

[4] This palindrome actually works better in the original
Greek than in this transliteration using our own alphabet.
This is because the *ps* in the first and last words of this
sentence are represented by a single Greek letter, *psi,*
or ψ.

INDO-EUROPEAN **OKW-,** "eye," has many other optical offspring. In Latin, **OKW-** gave rise to *oculus,* meaning "eye," the source of English *monocle,* or "one-eye," and *binoculars,* "two-eyes." In ancient Rome the word *oculus* also meant "bud," just as in English a potato's "bud" is called an *eye.* (Rose growers today use the term "blind" to refer to a stem without a bud or blossom.) From Latin *oculus* also came the Romans' word that means "to graft a bud from one tree to another," *inoculare*—the source of the medical term for implanting the "bud" of a disease, *inoculation.*

Another of **OKW-**'s many offspring is the Latin stem *-ox,* meaning "sight" or "appearance." When added to Latin *ferus,* "wild" (as in *feral* and *fierce*), *-ox* formed Latin *ferox,* or "wild-looking," the predecessor of English *ferocious.* Similarly, when *-ox* was added to Latin *ater,* or "black," the result was Latin *atrox,* a "dark, gloomy, dreadful appearance" —the source of the English word *atrocious.*

Latin *ater,* by the way, was part of the Romans' expression *dies atri,* or "black days." The Roman Senate applied this designation to certain dates on which some calamity had befallen the empire. On such days it was forbidden to conduct legal or political business. The Romans kept track of these *dies atri* by marking them on the calendar with a piece of coal. (In medieval times, "unlucky days" were called *dies mali,* or in Latin, "evil days."

53

This expression now lurks within the English word *dismal.*)

To return once again to the daisy's "eye": Indo-European **OKW-,** as noted earlier, is also the source of English *eye.* This name for the organ of sight now applies to several other things that resemble it, such as the *eyes* of Swiss cheese and the *eye* of a needle. (Russians, however, insert their thread into a needle's "little ear," or *ushko.*[5] Similarly, Germans stick their thread into the *Nadelöhr,* or "needle ear.") Also kin to **OKW-** and *eye* is *pigsney,* which means "darling" or "sweetheart," and comes from Middle English *piggesnye,* or literally, "pig's eye." This term of endearment, says the inimitable *OED,* probably originated "in children's talk and the fond prattle of nurses."

Yet another product of **OKW-** is French *oeil,* or "eye," which is now part of several English borrowings, such as *trompe l'oeil,* a style of painting in which objects are rendered in such exact detail that they seem real. We also have the French to thank for the loanword *oeillade,* "an amorous glance," which

• •

[5] *Ushko* calls to mind a marvelous Russian idiom involving ears—one that means roughly the same thing as "Don't try to put something over on me" or "Don't pull my leg." Literally, the expression *Ne veshay lapshu na ushi* means "Don't hang noodles from my ears."

is kin to English *ogle.* The English word *inveigle,* "to win over by deceitful enticement or flattery," comes from an Old French descendant of **OKW-**, *aveugle,* which is thought to come from a term meaning "without eyes." Also via French comes *ullage,* another picturesque derivative of **OKW-** that means "the amount of liquid that seeps out during transit or storage." *Ullage* comes from an Old French phrase that means "to fill a barrel up to the *oeil"*— in other words, up to its bunghole, or "eye."

DAISY

· · ·

The English word *window* is adapted from Old Norse *vindauga,* or literally, "wind-eye," from **OKW-**. (The word *wind* itself hails from another interesting word family: It's from the Indo-European root **WĒ-**, "to blow," which gave us *weather, ventilate, vent,* and Spanish *ventana,* "window." This root's Sanskrit descendant, *vāti,* "he blows," was joined to the prefix *nis-,* "out," to form the term for the concept of the "extinction of individual existence"—the "blowing out" also known as *Nirvana.*)

While we're gazing at *window,* we should also observe that in German a window is a *Fenster,* and in French, a *fenêtre,* both of which come from the Latin for "window," *fenestra.* This word is also part of English *fenestration,* "the pattern of windows on a building," and *defenestration,* the act of "throwing someone or something out a window." One last word about windows: *oeil-de-boeuf.* This French expression was adopted intact into English as the name of a style of circular window. *Oeil-de-boeuf* means "ox-eye," which also happens to be the name of a type of daisy.

Having returned to daisies, let us conclude with a brief look at the French and Spanish names for this flower, which offer some etymological surprises of their own. In Spain a daisy is a *margarita;* in France, it's a *marguerite.* Yet both these words also mean "pearl." This latter sense is illustrated by a children's ditty cited in Suzanne Brock's charming book of foreign phrases, *Idiom's Delight.*

> *Although my name is Marguerite,*
> *And Marguerite means pearl,*
> *No one thinks that I am sweet—*
> *For I'm the middle girl.*

Similarly, there's a Spanish proverb that warns against throwing *margaritas* to swine, but it has nothing to do with pelting pigs with petals or showering swine with salty cocktails. This advice refers instead to the biblical admonition against casting "pearls before swine."

How Spanish *margarita* and French *marguerite* came to mean both "pearl" and "daisy" is an intriguing question. Both words appear to stem from the Greek word for "pearl," *margaritēs,* which is itself of obscure origin. Some scholars say the link reflects either the resemblance between pearls and daisy buds, or perhaps the pearly lustre of daisy petals. This curious connection seems to be reflected in Sanskrit as well, where *manjarī* can mean either "pearl" or "a cluster of blossoms," and its etymological relative *manju* means "beautiful."

DAISY
• • •

In English, oddly enough, both *pearl* and *daisy* can be used to designate the same thing—namely, something considered "the best of its kind," as in "a pearl of great price," and "he's a real daisy." Furthermore, some etymologists say that the English word *doozy,* meaning "an extraordinary one of its kind," may be an altered form of *daisy.* (Others, however, maintain that *doozy* is a corruption of *Duesie,* an exceptionally fine car produced from 1921 to 1937 by Fred and Audie Duesenberg.) In Portuguese, the phrase *Pérola Negra,* or "Black Pearl," is an affectionate nickname for the man who may be the world's most famous athlete, Edson Arantes do Nascimento. Outside his native Brazil, the "Black Pearl" is better known as Pelé—not to be confused, of course, with Pele, the Hawaiian volcano goddess.

As we approach the end of this discussion of daisies, days, and eyes, let us also consider a string of derivatives from the Greek word *margaritēs.* There's the archaic English word for "pearl," *margarite,* which is now the name of a pearly, translucent mineral. A trace of the Greek word for "pearl" is also found in many kitchens: *Margarine* is so named because one of the acids used in its production forms a "pearly" sheen. This *margaritiferous* or "pearl-producing" family of words also includes the name *Margaret* as well as German *Gretchen,* or "little Margaret." The daisy, in fact, also goes by the English nicknames *Margaret, Margaret's herb,* and *Herb Margaret.*

Finally, the name of the infamous World War I spy *Mata Hari* also contains an intriguing etymological tangle that involves pearls, daisies, margarites, and Margarets: It seems *Mata Hari*'s real name was Gertrud *Margarete* Zelle. Whether by intent or accident, Gertrud Margarete Zelle chose for herself a name that in the Malay language means "sun" or "dawn"—or, if translated literally, *eye of the day.*

Dandelion

*D*espite this weed's sunny appearance, the *dandelion* has a rather ferocious name. It comes from French *dent de lion,* a literal rendering of this plant's Medieval Latin name, *dens leonis,* or "lion's tooth." This name refers, of course, to the way a dandelion's leaves resemble the toothy snarl of a lion. For several hundred years, in fact, the dandelion also went by the English nickname *lion's tooth.*

In venturing a closer look at this "lion's tooth," we'll meet several toothy terms, such as *indentation, al dente,* and *orthodontia,* as well as several linguistic relatives of *lion,* including the word *leopard* and, surprisingly enough, *chameleon.* We'll also take a look at some of the stranger nicknames for this weed, inspired by two of the dandelion's most distinctive characteristics.

THE *dan-* in *dandelion,* as well as French *dent* and Latin *dens,* comes from the Indo-European root **DENT-,** or "tooth." This root also produced English *dental, dentist, trident* ("three-toothed pitchfork"), and the "bite" taken from the beginning of a paragraph, the *indentation.*

DENT- is also part of the ancient Greek stem *odont-,* "tooth." When added to the Greek word for "breast," *mastos* (as in *mastectomy* and *mastitis*), this stem forms the name of the *mastodon,* a prehistoric beast named for the nipplelike protuberances on its molars. Greek *odont-* is also in *orthodontia,* or "tooth-straightening."[1]

DANDELION

. . .

   DENT- also left its mark in several modern languages. The Italian word for "tooth," *dente,* is part of the pasta-cooking term *al dente,* or "to the tooth" —in other words, "not overdone." The Spanish word for "tooth," *diente,* is another that doubles as a culinary term: Spanish cookbooks call for using a *diente* from a *cabeza* of garlic—that is, a "tooth" from a "head" of garlic.[2] Speaking of food, many scholars think that **DENT-** itself may come from an older prehistoric root called Indo-European **ED-,** which means "to bite." **ED-** is also the source of such English words as *eat, edible, obese, esurient* (which means "hungry" or "greedy"), and *etching,*

. . . .

[1] Greek *orthos,* meaning "straight" or "correct," is also part of *orthodoxy,* "correct opinion," and *orthography,* either "correct spelling" or "correct writing." Similarly, the name *orthopedics* originally applied to the branch of surgery that specialized in correcting deformities in *pediatric* cases.

[2] One is reminded of the English word *pilgarlic,* which means "a bald-headed man," and thus "a man regarded with mock pity," "a 'poor soul.' " The *pil-* in *pilgarlic* is thought to be related to *peeled,* the connection being the resemblance between a peeled head of garlic and a bald head.

an engraving made by using corrosive material to eat away a metal surface—a process that artists call "biting the plate."

THE source of the *lion* in *dandelion* is far more elusive. The word *lion* has cognates in many languages, including Spanish *león,* Portuguese *leão,* Italian *leone,* and Romanian *leu.* Scholars have tracked these names as far back as Latin *leo* and its Greek equivalent, *leōn.* Beyond that, these words' origins are unclear, although many experts surmise that they stem from a Semitic language.

It is certain, however, that Greek *leōn* now stalks about in several modern words. To *leōn* the ancient Greeks added their word for "earth" or "on the ground," *khamai,* to form the name of the humble lizard they called the "ground-lion"—or "dwarf lion," in other words—a name that led to this creature's English name, *chameleon.* (Greek *khamai,* by the way, belongs to a marvelous family of "earthy" words stemming from the Indo-European root **DHGHEM-.** From this source comes Latin *humus,* "earth," now found in English *humus* and *exhume,* to "take out of the earth." This root also produced the word *human,* or literally, "earthling"—a thought that is certainly *humbling,* yet another derivative of **DHGHEM-.**) The Greek word for "lion" is also in the name of another *leonine* animal, the *leopard,* once thought to be the offspring of a lion and the pantherlike cat called a *pard.*

Greek *leōn* lurks also within the botanical name of the flower called *leontopodium,* or "lion's foot." This name was previously applied to another genus of flowers that have a distinctive structure resembling a lion's paw. Botanists later transferred this name to the "small and white, clean and bright" blossom known as *edelweiss,* from German for "noble white." In Germany, by the way, the word for "lion" is *Löwe,* as in *Löwenbräu,* or "lion's brew," the beer whose label features a likeness of a lion.

DANDELION

· · ·

ALTHOUGH the English name *dandelion* evolved from a French phrase for "lion's tooth," the French use an entirely different name for this plant. In France a dandelion is a *pissenlit.* The *-lit* in this name is French for "bed," and the *piss-* is exactly what it sounds like. The name *pissenlit* stems from the fact that dandelion roots were once commonly dried and ground to mix with coffee. The dandelion, as one nineteenth-century medical text put it, possesses "unquestionably diuretic powers"—powers that could have untimely effects. In England and parts of the United States, the dandelion was once regularly called *pissabed,* and devotees gathered dandelion greens for a dish that went by the unappetizing name of *pissabed salad.* A folk tradition persists in both countries that someone who picks a dandelion will wet the bed that night.

As long as we're here, a brief survey of French *lit*

—the "bed," not the college course—will reward the effort. *Lit* (pronounced "lee") comes from Indo-European **LEGH-,** "to lie or lay." From the same root comes *lair,* the place where one "lies down." In Scotland this idea of "lying down" is carried a bit farther; there the word *lair* can also mean "cemetery plot." [3] **LEGH-** also produced the English words *law,* "something set down," as well as *leaguer,* "a military encampment," and thus *beleaguered,* "under siege."

LEGH-'s French descendant, *lit,* is also found in English *coverlet,* something that literally "covers a bed." *Lit,* interestingly enough, is kin to *litter,* a word that has a wonderfully vivid and logical history: *Litter* first meant "bed" or "portable couch," then "bedding material" such as straw or cedar chips, and eventually "the number of young brought forth" upon such bedding material. This sense of *litter* now has been extended to mean "a disorderly scattering," or, in other words, "a mess."

EACH of those bristly tufts on a mature dandelion, by the way, is called a *pappus,* from Greek *pappos,* meaning "grandfather" or "old man," because of the

. . . .

[3] Similarly, English *cemetery* comes from a family of Greek words that refer to the idea of "lying down" or "putting to sleep." A still more poetic—and comforting—term for "cemetery" is the Cherokee *tsu-na-da-ni-soh-di,* or literally, "they are laid there by others, not finally."

tufts' resemblance to a downy beard. This brings us to a final, strangely picturesque nickname for the dandelion, *monk's head*—a reference to the "bald pate" that remains at the top of a dandelion stem after all the seeds have been blown off.

DANDELION

. . .

Geranium

*B*ring your ear close to a *geranium* and you may hear the distant cry of a crane. This leggy, long-necked bird was known to the ancient Greeks as a *geranos,* and its derivative, *geranion,* was applied to the flower whose long, pointed seed pods resemble a crane's beak. *Geranion* later was adapted into the Latin word *geranium.*

Both English *crane* and Greek *geranos* hatched from the Indo-European root **GERƏ-2,** meaning "to cry hoarsely." In fact, **GERƏ-2** gave rise to a whole flock of cacophonous words, including such bird words as *crow, crake,* and *grackle,* and the noisy verbs *crack, croak,* and *croon.*

This Indo-European root also produced the Latin word for "crane," *grus,* now familiar to astronomers as the name of a constellation. Latin *grus* waded into a number of other languages as well, including French, where a crane is called a *grue.* French *grue* left its footprint in the English language in a most unexpected way: In Old French, the expression *pie de grue,* or "crane's foot," meant the three-line, claw-like mark denoting successive generations in a family tree. Speakers of English inherited this picture of a crane's foot or in the genealogical term *pedigree.*

. . .

THE crane's foot visible in the word *pedigree* isn't the only part of this lanky bird's anatomy that protrudes from other words. The crane's long beak inspired both the Greeks' name for the geranium, and an English nickname for this flower, *cranesbill*. A similar idea appears in German, where the geranium goes by the delicious name *Storchschnabel*, or "storksbill."[1] The crane's long, pointed bill also led the Romans to apply their name *grus*, or "crane," to a type of battering ram. (Another type of Roman battering ram was called, appropriately enough, an *aries*.)

The crane's distinctive neck prompted the Greeks to apply the name *geranos* to a type of pulley system used in theatrical productions. Similarly, in English the name *crane* also applies to a "long-necked" machine used for lifting. Similarly, in German this bird is a *Kranich*, and the long-necked machine is a *Kran*.

· ·

[1] Scientifically speaking, the popular window-box flowers commonly called *geraniums* are not true members of the *Geranium* genus. These so-called "geraniums" are officially classified as *pelargoniums*, from Greek *pelargos*, "stork," again, because of their beaklike seed pods. This is one of the many instances in which flower names tend to overlap and confuse. Consider that in English the flower name *storksbill*, which is often applied to the *pelargoniums*, can also be used to designate yet another plant —this one belonging to the genus *Erodium*, from Greek *erōdios*, "heron."

(In Germany, the word *Kran* also means "water faucet"—again a reference to a crane's neck.)

The image of this bird's neck may also be preserved in English *cranberry*. Some etymologists believe that this Thanksgiving staple is named for its slender, curved stems, which resemble the neck of a crane. A more likely explanation, however, is that these tangy berries thrive in exactly the type of boggy, marshy area frequented by cranes—an explanation supported by the fact that cranberries are also called *marsh-berries* and *fen-berries*.

GERANIUM

· · ·

The color of the crane's feathers is memorialized in the English expression *crane gray,* which is, according to Webster's, "a purplish gray that is bluer and duller than dove gray, bluer and slightly less strong than granite, darker and slightly redder than zinc, and bluer and darker than cinder gray." The *crane-fly,* which looks like an overgrown mosquito, is so named for its long, spindly legs. (A similar image is visible in the charming Dutch word for the crane-fly: In Holland this insect goes by the delightful name *langpootmug,* or literally, "long-foot-midge.")

THROUGH the millennia, the bird variously known as *geranos, grus, Kran,* and *crane* has been the subject of some intriguing tales—as has its namesake, the geranium. In Moslem tradition this brilliant flower was originally a drab weed. One day Muhammad draped his shirt over one of these lowly plants while

69

he bathed, and the geranium was miraculously transformed into a vivid blossom with a spicy aroma.

In Greek myth, it was a flock of cranes that warned Zeus' son Megarus that his father was so disgusted with human wickedness he planned to send torrential rains to cleanse the earth—a motif repeated throughout ancient myth. Young Megarus heeded the birds' advice and hurried off to *Mount Gerania,* thus surviving the devastating flood.

Cranes also have a walk-on role in the *Iliad.* Book Three contains a passing reference to a long series of wars between cranes and some legendary inhabitants of North Africa—people the Greeks believed were no taller than a human forearm. These yearly battles between the cranes and Pygmies were said to be particularly clamorous, although the poem never does explain what it was that had ruffled the feathers of either army in the first place.

In Japanese folklore, cranes live for a thousand years, and it is said that a sick person who folds a thousand origami cranes will be healed. This belief is reflected in the story of Sadako Sasaki, who like many other young survivors of the Hiroshima bombing, developed leukemia. Undaunted, the girl determined to fold a thousand paper cranes, and finished 644 of them before her death. Friends folded the remaining cranes, and the tiny figures were buried with her body. Today in Hiroshima Peace Park a statue of Sadako Sasaki commemorates the children who died in the attack, and each year on the August

6 anniversary of the bombing, the statue is showered with thousands of paper cranes.

GERANIUM

. . .

Finally, from the traditions of Central Mexico comes a familiar word that also preserves within itself the image of a long, leggy crane. The name of the *Aztecs* is said to commemorate the legendary site of their origin. This place was called *Aztlan,* a name that in Nahuatl means "near the crane"—which is quite a pedigree indeed.

Gladiolus

*T*o the ancient Romans, a *gladius* was a sword, and a little sword was a *gladiolus.* The Roman author Pliny the Elder applied the latter word to a flower that is distinguished by its long, sword-shaped leaves—and the name has stuck.

Scholars have traced the Latin word *gladius* and its diminutive *gladiolus* to an Indo-European root called **KEL-1,** which means "to strike" or "cut." **KEL-1** is thought to be the source of a number of words that involve "cutting" or "striking," including *iconoclast, coup, claymore,* and surprisingly enough, *clematis.*

Those in antiquity who lived and died by the *gladius* for the entertainment of others were called *gladiatores.* Actually, however, in order to lend variety to the Coliseum's grisly spectacle, the *gladiators,* as they are now known in English, were divided into many types, and not all of them used swords. The *retiarius,* for example, ran about the arena with a trident, a dagger, and a net—in Latin, a *rete*—trying to snare, then stab, his opponents. (Latin *rete* and *retiarius* are closely related to the "net" in one's eye known as the *retina,* and the drawstring purse called a *reticule,* or "little net.") Similarly, the arsenal of the *laqueator* included a *laqueus,* or "noose," traces of which are found in the Spanish loan word *lasso* and in the English word *lace,* which first denoted a "cord," then an "ornamental braid," and eventually "delicate meshwork."

THE "cutting" and "striking" root **KEL-1** also carved out a place in the ancient Greek language in such words as *klan,* "to break" and *klasis,* "a breaking." Stemming from these words is the *-clast* in English iconoclast, originally someone who strikes at a religious *icon* (from Greek *eikōn,* "image"). When *iconoclastic* ideas are too threatening, some people and governments become *biblioclasts,* or "destroyers or mutilators of books." A more productive kind of cutting is represented by *osteoclasis,* a medical term for breaking a bone in order to correct it surgically.[1]

KEL-1 also produced the ancient Greek word *klōn,* meaning "twig," or literally, "something that breaks off." *Klōn* now pokes through the modern English word for "genetic offshoot," *clone.* Another of **KEL-1**'s offspring is Greek *klēma,* meaning

· ·

[1] Someone who performs such procedures had better be good at *algebra,* since the first definition for *algebra* listed in the *OED* is "The surgical treatment of fractures; bone-setting." The word *algebra* comes from Arabic *al jebr,* "the reunion of broken parts," from *jabara,* "unite." Thus this old expression for "bone-setting" shares a name with the branch of mathematics that involves "reuniting" the "broken parts" of an equation.

"twig" or "branch." A form of this word became the name of the twiggy plant the Greeks called *Klēmatis,* now known as *clematis.*

Another word that apparently comes from **KEL-1** —and thus is another relative of *gladiolus* and its cutting kin—is the Greek *kolaphos,* "a blow with the fist" or "a box on the ear." This word's Latin counterpart, *colaphus,* eventually found its way into French as *coup,* meaning a "blow" or "stroke." This word provided several useful phrases that were borrowed directly into English: *coup d'etat,* literally a "stroke of state"; *coup de grace,* a "stroke of mercy" or "death blow"; *coup d'oeil,* literally, "a stroke of the eye," which refers to a glance that takes in a whole scene at once. In English the word *coup* itself now means "a clever, highly successful stratagem," as in the marketing *coup* that scores a "hit" with customers. Speaking of marketing, it's no coincidence that those redeemable certificates framed by a dotted line to make them easier to cut out are called *coupons.*

The kindred French verb *couper,* "to cut," produced the name of the car called a *coupe.* The original expression was *carrosse coupé,* or "cut-off coach," which referred to a vehicle with a closed compartment for passengers and an outside seat for the driver. One last derivative of Latin *colaphus* is *cope,* originally "to come to blows with." Gradually *cope* acquired the meaning of "contend with" or "match." Now the word *cope* seems to

GLADIOLUS
. . .

75

be used most often by those who are convinced they can't.

The same root that gave the Romans *gladius* and *gladiolus* produced sword-words in several other languages. **KEL-1,** for example, led to the archaic English word *glaive,* or "broadsword." It also shows up in Welsh *cleddyf,* "sword," and in the Gaelic expression *claidheamh mōr,* or "great sword," the source of English *claymore,* a double-edged broadsword. (The *mōr,* or "great," in *claidheamh mōr,* by the way, is a cognate of English *more* and *most,* as well as Welsh *mawr,* "big," as in *Bryn Mawr,* or "Big Hill.")

You may never have felt it, but there's also a little sword in your chest. The *gladiolus* in anatomical nomenclature is the long middle section of the sternum or breastbone. In keeping with this image, the sternum's upper section is called the *manubrium,* the Latin word for "handle." This word comes from Latin *manus,* "hand," which has also handed down such words as *manipulate, manufacture, manicotti* ("little sleeves" of pasta), as well as *maneuver* (from Latin *manu operari,* "to work by hand"), and *maneuver's* close relative, *manure* (from Old French *manouvrer,* to "work by hand"—in other words, "to cultivate" or "till.")

At the lower end of the "little sword" in your chest is the pointed tip of cartilage known as the *xiphoid process,* an anatomical landmark familiar to those trained in cardiopulmonary resuscitation. English *xiphoid,* or "swordlike," comes from the Greek word for "sword," *xiphos*—which, as every Scrabble player should know, is the source of an English word for "swordfish," *xiphias.*

While we're on the subject of anatomy, we should also note that when an ancient Roman thrust his *gladius* back into his scabbard, he was said to be putting his sword back into his *vagina.* This Latin word for "sheath"—which in antiquity probably sounded more like "wahgeenah"—inspired the English term for what one prudish writer termed "that portal through which a child enters the world."

The double meaning of Latin *vagina* was well known to the Romans. This of course led to some rather crude puns, as in a comedy by Plautus, when a young man is teased by someone who asks, *"Noctu in vigiliam quando ibat miles, quo tu ibas simul, conveniebatne in vaginam tuam machaera militis?"* Roughly translated, this reads, "At night when the soldier went on his watch and you went with him, was the guy's sword a good fit for your scabbard?" (In this case, the playwright used another Latin word for sword, *machaera.*)

Not surprisingly, the Romans sometimes used *gladius* as a synonym for the male organ—that is, in addition to such typically Roman names as *clava,* "club," and *vomer,* "plow," as well as *penis,* which could also mean "tail." (For more about this, see the chapter on **Anthurium**.) I should hasten to add here that Latin *gladius* is not, as one might suspect, the

77

source of modern English *glad.* This word comes from an entirely different Indo-European root, **GHEL-2,** which shines through several "bright" English words including *gleam, glimmer, glisten, glare, glaze, gloaming* (a poetic word for "twilight"), and *glee.*

The flower name *gladiolus* also inspired the name of another blossom, the *gladdon,* a type of iris. This name usually applies to the flower botanists call *Iris foetidissima,* the "very fetid" or "stinking" iris—and with good reason, because this gladdon may gladden the eye, but not the nose.

In fact, both the iris and the gladiolus are close botanical relatives. They belong to the Iris family, which includes several different flowers with xiphoid, or "sword-shaped," leaves, such as the Spanish iris, or, as it is known to botanists, *Xiphium iris.* The close connection between these flowers is also reflected in German, where a gladiolus is a *Gladiole,* and an iris is a *Schwertlilie,* or "sword lily"; in English, however, the name *sword lily* is applied not to the iris, but to the gladiolus.

Confused? No matter. The bottom line is this: If you're feeling the least bit belligerent, you can say so —and ever so politely—by sending someone a "little sword" or gladiolus. If your recipient is etymologically astute, he or she will be sure to get the point.

Hyacinth

he name of the *hyacinth* commemorates one of the world's oldest homosexual love affairs. In Greek myth, Hyacinth was a young prince of Sparta, an exceptionally handsome fellow of whom both Apollo and Zephyrus, god of the west wind, were enamored. There was yet a third rival for Hyacinth's affections, the mortal poet Thamyris. As things turned out, however, poor Thamyris was eliminated from the competition early on, having made the fatal mistake of boasting that his own singing surpassed even that of the Greek muses. Apollo relayed this information to the goddesses, who in turn robbed Thamyris of his voice, eyesight, and musical talent—a response that shouldn't have been surprising, given the thoroughly Greek belief that human hubris inevitably invites divine retribution.

Hyacinth, meanwhile, chose to return the attentions of Apollo, much to the chagrin of Zephyrus. Not long after, the west wind god chanced upon the happy couple as they were taking turns throwing the discus. Enraged, Zephyrus caught the discus in a gust of wind and sent it crashing into Hyacinth's skull, killing him on the spot. Apollo, overcome with grief for his mortal lover, fashioned a purple flower from drops of the young man's blood, and in his honor the Greeks called this flower *huakinthos.*

HYACINTH

· · ·

Several ancient writers claimed that the petals of *huakinthos* bore markings that resembled the Greek letters alpha and iota, which spelled *Ai,* the ancient Greek word for "alas." There is some question as to whether such markings can be discerned on any of the flowers now commonly called *hyacinths.* Nevertheless, this belief has persisted through the centuries, inspiring many literary allusions. The poet Milton, for example, called the hyacinth "that sanguine flower inscribed with woe."

The ancient Greeks later applied the name of this purple flower to a precious blue stone, most likely the sapphire. Similarly, the modern English word *hyacinth* applies not only to a flower, but also to a ruddy orange gemstone, often called *jacinth,* a name adapted from *hyacinth.* (Similarly, the French word *jacinthe* can refer either to the flower or the gem.)

THE *-inthos* ending the Greek name of the hyacinth is a rarity in that language, suggesting that this word is from a non-Indo-European source, and lending credence to the belief that the story of this flower's origin is a corrupted version of a far earlier myth. The young Hyacinth seems to have been associated with the "vegetation" deities widely worshipped by non-Indo-European peoples who inhabited that part of the world long before the Greeks arrived on the scene. His story reflects a motif repeated throughout ancient myth, that of the handsome youth who dies and is mourned by a divine being—a story symbolizing the yearly cycle of lush springtime growth, followed by ripening and withering in the blazing heat of summer. In early Crete, Hyacinth was worshipped as a god of flowers, and his death was bewailed each spring by a goddess. In Sparta the annual commemoration of his death, held in the early summer month called *Hyacinthius,* was considered that nation's second-most important festival. It was a three-day affair that began with grieving for the fallen youth and gradually changed to a celebration of the might and majesty of Apollo.

For what it's worth, the ancients also believed that the hyacinth's bulbous root held the power to postpone a boy's puberty, possibly because Hyacinth's own progress toward adulthood was arrested so suddenly. Perhaps it's no accident, then, that in medieval England people commonly believed that drinking a mixture of mashed hyacinth bulbs and white wine hindered the growth of facial hair.

ALTHOUGH Zephyrus played villain in the story of hapless young Hyacinth, this cruel and lusty god was more or less rehabilitated as time went on. In early Greek myth, he was a vengeful deity who delighted in fomenting deadly storms at sea. When he desired the gracious flower goddess *Chlōris* (or "greenness," as in *chlorophyll,* or "green-leaf"), Zephyrus did

what came naturally to gods in such cases—he kidnapped her. He also had a fling with one of the
Harpies, those monsters with the faces of women
and the bodies of birds. As so often happens in ancient myth, this unlikely union resulted in equally
unlikely offspring: a pair of horses.

HYACINTH
. . .

Zephyrus also begat some linguistic offspring as
well. The lovely-sounding ancient Greek expression
zephuria ova means "putrid eggs laid in springtime,"
and stems from the Greeks' belief that if an egg was
soft-shelled or otherwise rotten, it must not have
been fathered by an animal but by the wind itself.
The same idea is tucked into the English term *wind-
egg*, which as the *OED* suggests, can be used to devastating effect, as when an early nineteenth-century
critic groused, "Here is a Dr. Raupach who lays a
tragedy or two in the year—mostly wind-eggs."

Over time, Zephyrus mellowed. In later Greek
myth, he personified the fragrant wind wafting over
the Elysian fields, home of the blessed in the afterlife.[1] In modern English *zephyr* has come to mean "a
mild, gentle wind." In fact, William Shakespeare
conjured the very picture of mildness by invoking

. . . .

[1] These fields, by the way, were said to be carpeted with the
type of flower the Greeks called the *asphodelos*. Somewhere along the way, a later version of this flower's name
acquired an initial *d* sound, and formed the name of the
flower known in English as the *daffodil.*

this linguistic descendant of the blustering god of the west wind:

> They are as gentle as zephyrs
> blowing below the violet, not wagging
> his sweet head.

Hydrangea

he flowery clusters called *hydrangeas* take their name from two Greek words that mean "water vessel," because their seed pods resemble tiny cups. The "water" (or in Greek, *hudōr*) in the hydrangea's name is among many watery words that spilled forth from a single Indo-European root meaning "water," or "wet." This family of words includes such seemingly unlikely cousins as *hydrogen, whiskey, vodka, otter,* and *Vaseline.* The "vessel"—or in Greek, *angeion*—in *hydrangea* has only a few English relatives, most of which are used primarily in the field of science.

Because there are so many "water" words to consider, let's first dispense with the "vessel" within this blossom's name: In addition to giving us the *-angea* in *hydrangea,* Greek *angeion* also inspired the English word *angiosperms,* the scientific term for those flowering plants that bear their "seed," or *sperma,* within an ovary or "vessel." (In contrast, the seeds of *gymnosperms,* such as the cone-bearing pine or fir trees, are exposed, or in Greek, *gumnos,* "naked." Greek *gumnos,* is also found in the name of the places where ancient athletes trained, a *gymnasium.*)

The Greeks also applied the word *angeion* to various "vessels" or "cavities" in the human body. As a result, the study of vessels that carry blood and lymph is now known as *angiology,* and the medical treatment that involves inflating a tiny balloon to open clogged arteries is called *angioplasty,* or literally, "vessel-spreading." (The *-plasty* in *angioplasty* comes from the Greek verb *plassein,* meaning to "spread out," or "to mold." This verb also produced English *plaster, plastic,* and the term for the "molding" or remodeling of a nose, *rhinoplasty.*)

HYDRANGEA
. . .

Now on to the "water" in the hydrangea's name. Greek *hudōr* comes from an Indo-European root called **WED-1,** meaning "water" or "wet." Scholars suspect that Greek *hudōr* evolved from a suffixed form of this root, *ud-ōr.* This Greek word for "water," in turn, produced several modern English words.

Greek *hudōr* is part of such words as *Hydra,* the name of a many-headed water serpent in ancient Greek myth. Heracles' famous Twelve Labors included killing the Hydra, an endeavor which at first seemed hopeless, because each time one of the monster's heads was chopped off, several more grew in its place. In English the word *hydra* now serves as a metaphor denoting any complicated problem that poses new obstacles whenever one aspect of it is solved. The scientific name *Hydra* applies to a tiny freshwater polyp capable of generating new offspring from its severed parts. The word *hydra* is also an etymological relative of the name of another water

animal, the *otter*, another derivative of **WED-1.** The linguistic link between the names for these animals is more clearly seen in the cognates of English *otter*, including Lithuanian *ūdras*, Latvian *udrs*, and Sanskrit *udrās*.

Having too much water in one's body is a key symptom of an ailment that the Greeks called *hudropsis*. In English the name for this condition has been shortened to *dropsy*. The Greek word for "water" is also found inside fire *hydrants*, which are sometimes opened in the summertime by people who feel *dehydrated*. The water that pours from those hydrants is composed of one part oxygen and two parts *hydrogen*—the latter element having taken its name from the French term *hydrogène*, or literally, "water-generating." (Similarly, the name *oxygen* is taken from the Greek word *oxus*, meaning "sharp" or "acrid," and was named for its "acid-generating" ability. This peculiar quality is probably more obvious in the German word for "oxygen," *Sauerstoff*, or literally, "sour-stuff.") [1]

The Greeks also added *hudōr* to their word for "silver," *arguros*, to form their name for the element mercury, *hudrarguros*. The Latin version of this name, *hydrargyrum*, led to the modern chemical symbol for mercury, *Hg*. (In Latin this element was also

· ·

[1] Greek *oxus*, or "sharp," is also part of the word that denotes a "pointedly foolish" statement, *oxymoron*, about which more is found in the chapter on **Orchid.**

called *argentum vivum,* or "living silver." This expression inspired both the French term for "mercury," *vif-argent,* and the English synonym *quicksilver*—the *quick,* in this case, meaning "alive," as in the phrases "the quick and the dead" and "cut to the quick.")

HYDRANGEA

. . .

Greek *arguros* is among several fascinating words that descended from the Indo-European root **ARG-,** which means "to shine." This illustrious group includes such members as English *argil* (a clay that becomes bright white when fired), French *argent* ("silver" or "money"), and *Argentina* (the "silvery" land).

Another descendant of **ARG-,** surprisingly enough, is English *argue*—which originally meant "to make clear," even though often it now seems that arguments have the opposite effect. This is especially true when lawyers are doing the arguing, which is precisely why it's high time to rescue from obscurity yet another water word, *clepsydra.* The clepsydra was a type of water clock used in the law courts of ancient Athens to limit the length of arguments. Its name literally means "water-thief," and comes from the Greek words *hudōr* and *kleps,* or "thief" (as in *kleptomaniac,* also spelled *cleptomaniac*). The clepsydra was a type of *angeion* or vessel that had small holes punctured in the bottom. It was filled with water, which then gradually trickled out, much like sand through an hourglass. Different amounts of water were allotted for different types of cases, and

89

when all the water had run out, so had the speaker's time.

Anyone who has a morbid fear of water is said to suffer from *hydrophobia.* The word *hydrophobia* also serves as a synonym for "rabies," the symptoms of which include an aversion to water and an inability to swallow. A lesser-known English synonym for rabies is *Lyssa,* a name inspired by an ancient Greek deity. In Greek myth, *Lussa* (or in Latinized form, *Lyssa*) was the goddess of madness. In some versions of the story, it was *Lussa,* for example, who provoked in Heracles such a rage that he mistook his wife and children for those of his bitterest enemy and killed them all. When he came to his senses, the hero did penance for his crimes by completing his dozen labors, which included, by the way, the killing of the Hydra. (Actually, many etymologists think the Greek word *lussa* itself belongs to a fascinating family of "wolf" words discussed at length in the chapter on **Lupine.**)

A close relative of Greek *lussa,* or "rabies," was *lutta,* a name given to what the ancients believed was a "little worm" under a dog's tongue. Pliny the Elder wrote that surgically removing this "worm" from puppies would prevent them from ever getting rabies.[2] (Today the Latinized version of this word,

· ·

[2] The dubious nature of such a prescription is reflected much later in Samuel Johnson's 1755 *Dictionary,* which offers this explanation for the expression *to worm:* "To

lytta, can be used in English to denote the thin, cartilaginous strip on the underside of a dog's tongue.)

Greek *lussa,* at any rate, also inspired a couple of modern English flower names. One of them, *antholyza,* is applied to a blossom that resembles the gaping jaws of a rabid dog. The word *lussa* is also found in the name of a flower that for centuries was believed to have the power to cure hydrophobia—the viral kind, that is. The same plant has gone by such names as *madwort* and *heal-dog.* This blossom is more widely known, however, by a name formed from the Greek prefix *a,* meaning "not," and *lussa,* which led to the name of the "anti-madness" flower called *alyssum.*

HYDRANGEA

• • •

BESIDES the name of the hydrangea, **WED-1**'s other watery offspring include English *wash, wet, wave,* and *winter* (the "wet" season). The same root inspired the Latin word for "wave," *unda,* which now sways inside such words as *undulate,* "to move in a wavelike manner," as well as *abundant* and *surround,* both of which suggest the idea of "overflowing," and *redundant,* literally, "overflowing back again."

WED-1 also led to the English word *water* itself, as well as its cognates in many languages, including

• • • • • • • • • • • • • • • • • • • •

deprive a dog of something, nobody knows what, under his tongue, which is said to prevent him, nobody knows why, from running mad."

Sanskrit *udán,* Lithuanian *vanduõ,* and German *Wasser.* (The German word for "water," incidentally, is part of some vivid linguistic compounds: The German word for "hydrogen" is *Wasserstoff,* or literally, "water-stuff," and thus an H-bomb is a *Wasserstoffbombe.* The German word for the zodiac sign Aquarius is *Wassermann,* the "water-bearer" or "water-pourer." German *Wasser* was combined with the Greek word for "oil," *elaion,* to form the trademark name, *Vaseline.*)

The Russian word for "water," *voda,* also comes from **WED-1.** By adding a diminutive ending to *voda,* the Russians formed their name for the drink they affectionately call "little water," *vodka.* In fact, it's not at all uncommon for speakers of various languages to "water down" their names for strong drinks. Latin *aqua vitae,* for example, literally means "water of life," but was long used as a synonym for "distilled spirits." In Scandinavia, *aqua vitae* became *aquavit* or *akvavit,* and was borrowed into English as the name of a type of liquor flavored with caraway seeds. Among the French, *eau de vie*—literally, "water of life"—is a synonym for "brandy." Latin *aqua vita* also flavored its Scottish and Irish Gaelic equivalent, *uisge beatha,* which over time evolved into *usquebaugh,* and eventually was imported into English as *whiskey.*

Anyway, if your own cup runneth over, you can always say so with an eloquent spray of hydrangeas.

Iris

Iris, in Greek myth, was the name of a versatile goddess who held a number of part-time jobs. As the swift-footed messenger goddess in *The Iliad,* she was "Iris, who runs on the rainy wind," flying along foamy seas, clad in brilliant, multicolored robes. Iris was also the divine personification of the rainbow, and it was said she could sometimes be seen after a rain gliding along the arc of many hues that formed her bridge between heaven and earth. The earliest Greek poets described Iris as a virgin goddess, a sister of the Harpies. In later poetry she was the wife of Zephyrus, the god of the west wind, and in some stories it is she who gave birth to Eros, the god of romantic love, from whose name we get the word *erotic.*

The ancient Romans revered Iris as the goddess who received the souls of dying women. She was also Juno's faithful messenger and personal attendant. (Shakespeare's Queen Margaret alludes to that relationship in *2 Henry VI,* telling a guest who is about to depart: "Let me hear from thee;/for wheresoe'er thou art in this world's globe,/I'll have an Iris that shall find thee out.") A devoted servant, Iris firmly resisted the advances of Juno's philandering husband, Jupiter. In gratitude Juno created a flower in her honor, whose blooms, like the shimmering robes of the goddess, span a wide range of colors.

IRIS

• • •

LIKE the rainbow goddess herself, the ancient Greek word *iris* came to serve several different functions. *Iris* referred not only to this beloved deity and to the rainbow itself, but also to the flower that honored her. The Greeks also used the word *iris* as a synonym for any iridescent garment, and eventually, for a "bright circle surrounding something," such as the halo of a candle or the rings around the "eyes" in a peacock's tail.

In modern English, of course, *iris* is commonly applied to the colored ring within, not around, an eye. *Iris* also was once regularly used as an English synonym for rainbow, as in Lord Byron's description of a sunset:

> Heaven is free
> From clouds, but of all colours seems to be,—
> Melted to one vast Iris of the West,—
> Where the day joins the past Eternity.

Similarly, the rain in Spain falls mainly prior to the appearance of an *arco iris* in the sky—an "Iris arc," in other words. In France a rainbow is an *arc-en-ciel,* or an "arc in the sky." In Germany the colorful aftermath of a rainstorm is called a *Regenbogen,* a cognate of *rainbow.*

In both French and Spanish the word *iris* applies not only to the ring of color in one's eye, but also to the flower, just as in English. In German, though, these two have entirely different names: The iris of the eye is a *Regenbogenhaut,* or literally, a "rainbow membrane." (German *Haut* means "membrane," "skin," or "peel," and shares a common ancestor with the English noun *hide.)* However, the German word for the iris growing in a garden is called a *Schwertlilie,* or "sword lily," due to its long, pointed leaves. (More about swords, irises, and the German word *Schwertlilie* can be found in the chapter on **Gladiolus.**)

THE name of the rainbow goddess, Iris, inspired a wide spectrum of linguistic derivatives. The English word *iridescent* describes something having rainbow-like colors, especially hues that shift with the light, such as those in pearls and opals. (Another wonderful adjective along these lines is English *chatoyant,* which is adapted from French *chatoyer,* "to shine like a cat's eyes.") The chemical element *iridium* is a white metal which, when dissolved in certain solutions, gives off a variety of colors. An *iridocyte* is a type of cell in fishes that creates a similar rainbowlike effect.

The flower named for "the various goddess of the rain-bow," as Alexander Pope called her, can also claim some linguistic progeny of its own. A variant form of *iris* is *orris,* which is found in *orrisroot,* the fragrant rootstock of certain irises, now used in many perfumes and cosmetics as well as in various orange-flavored liqueurs.

IRIS

· · ·

Vert d'iris, a borrowing of the French for "iris green," is a bright green pigment made from one species of iris, which once was popular among painters of miniatures. (Speaking of *miniature,* this word doesn't come directly from Latin *minimus,* meaning "smallest," as one might expect. Its roots are in the Latin word *minium,* the name of a red pigment formerly used to illuminate manuscripts with red letters. This word's similarity to Latin *minimus, minor* ("less"), and *minuere* ("diminish") apparently helped confuse the sense of *miniature,* so that the word came to be applied to a "small painting" and eventually to any "small replica."

Finally, in current usage *iris* has been adapted to cinematography. An *iris diaphragm* is not, as one might suspect, a contraceptive available in a wide variety of colors. Rather, it is the adjustable metal disk that forms the aperture of a camera or microscope and can be made wider or narrower, much as an iris in the eye responds to light. An *iris-in* is a moviemaking technique also known as a *film wipe.* When an image is irised-in, it grows outward from a small circle in the center of the screen. The reverse of this process, when the on-screen picture shrinks into a tiny dot, is an *iris-out,* which ends all those Looney Tunes pictures after Porky Pig sputters, "Th-th-th-th-th-th-that's all, folks!"

Lily

Consider the lilies, and you're in for a puzzle—at least from an etymological point of view. The name of the *lily* can be traced as far as the Latin word *lilium* and its Greek equivalent, *leirion,* but there the well-marked linguistic trail turns cold. This has led scholars to conclude that the Latin and Greek names were borrowed from a language other than Indo-European.

The English word *lily* has come to be something of a generic term applied loosely to several different flowers, not all of which belong to the large botanical group known as the Lily family, or *Liliaceae.* The most popular of these include the *day lily, Easter lily, calla lily,* and *tiger lily.* We'll consider these lilies later in this chapter, after we take a closer look at some of the names for the lily in the ancient world.

THE versatile English word *lily* proved handy for the translators of the King James Bible when they were seeking an equivalent for the Hebrew word *shōshannāh,* a flower name which also seems to have applied to several different types of blossoms. At various points in the erotic poetry of the Song of Songs, for example, the word *shōshannāh* may suggest a red blossom: "His cheeks are as a bed of

spices, as sweet flowers: his lips like lilies, dropping sweet smelling myrrh." Elsewhere in that book, however, the color of the sensuous *shōshannāh* is wide open to conjecture, as in these passages: "Thy two breasts are like two young roes that are twins, which feed among the lilies," and "Thy navel is like a round goblet, which wanteth not liquor; thy belly is like an heap of wheat set about with lilies."

The Hebrew flower name *shōshannāh* is preserved in the modern English names *Susan* and *Susannah*. (In Jewish lore, *Susannah* was a woman of lilylike purity who was falsely accused of adultery; ultimately her innocence prevailed.) For what it's worth, the Hebrew word for "lily" also inspired the Hungarian name *Zsa Zsa*.

The Latin word *lilium*—like its English offspring *lily* and its Hebrew equivalent *shōshannāh*—apparently have applied to several different flowers. The ancient Romans also adopted the word *lilium* into their military vocabulary, where it had a particularly grisly application: The Roman army's defenses included a series of trenches with rows of sharpened wooden stakes planted along the bottom, their points protruding about four inches above ground level and camouflaged with twigs and brushwood. In his commentaries on the Gallic War, Julius Caesar wrote of such a spike, *"Id ex similitudine floris, lilium appellabant"*: "Because of its resemblance to the flower, they called this a 'lily.' "

Latin *lilium* (in its more benign sense) is the

source of the word for "lily" in almost all Germanic and Romance languages, including German *Lilie,* Spanish *lirio,* and French *lis.* (French *fleur-de-lis,* or "lily flower," is probably a misnomer. According to many historians, this symbol of French royalty is modeled instead on the white iris.)

LILY

. . .

The Greek counterpart of Latin *lilium* is *leirion.* (*Leirion,* or "lily," by the way, is part of the marvelous ancient Greek word *leiriopolphanemōnē,* "an omelet made with lilies," a recipe that's not so outlandish, considering that the *Liliaceae* include such edible plants as asparagus.)

The word *leirion* was often used specifically for the brilliant white *Madonna lily,* named for its traditional association with the *Madonna* or Virgin Mary.[1] (The name *Madonna* is from Old Italian *ma donna,* or "my lady.") The Madonna lily's use as a sym-

. . . .

[1] A growing body of evidence suggests that this flower's connection with the Virgin is actually a relatively late manifestation of a long tradition linking the lily with the prehistoric mother goddesses of the ancient Near East. Standard biblical commentaries note that the so-called "lily" or *shōshannāh* of Hebrew scripture may be closely identified with the lotus, a flower well known as an extremely primitive and widespread symbol of the generative power of the Great Mother Goddess. In later Roman myth, the lily was the floral emblem of the mother goddess Juno, and it was said that when milk spurted from Juno's breasts to form the Milky Way, the drops that fell to earth became lilies.

bol of purity is also reflected in this flower's botanical name, *Lilium candidum.* Latin *candidum* means "dazzling white," and is a relative of such English words as *candle, incandescent, candor*— originally "purity," then later "freedom from malice or bias"—and *candidiasis,* a fungus infection that forms white patches on the inside of the mouth. *Candidum* is also kin to English *candidate,* a word inspired by would-be officeholders in ancient Rome who wore bright white togas in hopes of convincing voters of their pure character. These togas, which were bleached or rubbed with chalk to make them more convincing, earned such politicians the name *candidati.* (Such a vote-gathering effort, by the way, was called an *ambitio,* or literally, a "going-around" to seek support—from which comes the English word for what impels so many modern politicians to do the same, *ambition.*)

Besides the word *leirion,* the Greeks also used another word, *krinon,* which English translators usually render as "lily." A form of this word is used in the original Greek in the famous passage from the Gospel of Matthew:

> Consider the lilies of the field, how they grow; they toil not, neither do they spin: And yet I say unto you, that even Solomon in all his glory was not arrayed like one of these.

Although the Greek flower name *krinon* usually applied specifically to the *Lilium candidum,* or Madonna lily, most biblical scholars tend to believe that the "lilies" in this particular passage may have referred to any of several flowers that dot the hillsides of Palestine, including the poppy, gladiolus, iris, and scarlet martagon.

Whatever the exact meaning of Greek *krinon,* a trace of this word is now found in English *crinoid,* which describes certain sea creatures noted for their stalklike bodies and feathery arms. The *crinoids,* or "lilylike ones," include such lyrically named ocean dwellers as the *feather star* and the *sea lily.*

Now, to consider a few other lilies:

As its name suggests, the blossom of the *day lily* lasts for only a day. This tawny flower is classified in the botanical genus *Hemerocallis,* from Greek *hēmera,* "day," and *kallos,* "beauty." (Modern Greeks use a sort of backward version of this name for their traditional morning greeting: *"Kalēmera!"* "Good day!")

Greek *hēmera* is also in the English words *hemeralopia* ("day blindness"), *nycthemeron* (a period of time lasting "a day and a night"), *ephemeron* ("a short-lived organism or thing"), and *ephemeral,* which describes something "fleeting," such as the beauty of a day lily. (More about the *day* in *day lily* can be found in the chapter on **Daisy.**)

The *kallos* or "beauty" in the genus name *Hemer-ocallis* is found also in such lovely English words as *calligraphy* ("beautiful writing"), *kaleidoscope* (literally, "beautiful-form viewer"), and *callipygian,* which describes someone having "beautiful buttocks."

Greek *kallos* pretties up the names of several other flowers as well. The name *calliopsis,* or "beautiful appearance," is sometimes substituted for *coreopsis* to refer to this flower whose name reflects its seeds' "bedbuglike appearance." (More about *calliopsis* and *coreopsis* in the chapter on **Daisy**.) The pink orchid called *calopogon* is named for its yellow, beardlike structure, *pōgōn* being Greek for "beard," and also found in English *pogontrophy,* or "beard-growing," and *pogonotomy,* a rather grandiose term for "shaving." The distinctive *calla lily*—which really isn't a lily at all, but a member of the Arum family—is thought to come from Greek *kallaia,* "rooster's wattles," a bit of ornithological ornamentation which is yet another derivative of *kallos.*

The name *day lily* also applies to an entirely different plant, also known as the *plantain lily.* The *plantain* in its name comes from Latin *planta,* or "sole of the foot," a reference to this plant's broad, flat leaves. (Latin *planta* is also kin to English *plantar,* as in the *plantar wart* that appears on the sole of one's foot, and in the verb *plant,* from Latin *plantare,* "to push in with the foot when planting.") The plantain is also commonly known by its genus name *Hosta,* which commemorates the nineteenth-century Austrian botanist Nicolaus T. Host.

THE name *Easter lily* applies to several flowers, including the Madonna lily. These spectacular blossoms are so named for their traditional association with the Christian celebration of the Resurrection. The *Easter* in its name has a most instructive history: Early Christian missionaries discovered that the inhabitants of northern Europe regularly observed festive annual rites honoring the goddess of the dawn, known to some tribes as *Eostre* and to others as *Ostara.* These and other names for the "dawn goddess," including Latin *Aurora* and Greek *Ēōs,* are thought to derive from Indo-European **AUS-1,** which is also the source of the English words *east* and *eastern.*

The ceremonies held each spring to honor the goddess of the dawn were marked by joyous celebration. Children carried on the Germanic tradition of coloring eggs and searching for newborn rabbits, both activities associated with fertility and the renewal of life in the springtime. The existence of these yearly festivities proved quite convenient for the early church fathers, who quickly set about replacing the popular pagan rites with a celebration of their own god's resurrection.

. . .

FINALLY, the orange and black *tiger lily* is named, of course, for the way its coloration resembles those of the big striped cat. A Korean legend offers a charming explanation for this flower's origin. Long ago, a hermit with magic powers helped a tiger by removing an arrow from its leg. The two became friends, and when the animal died, the man changed him into a tiger lily so he would always be close at hand. Later the man drowned, and the lily spread far and wide in search of his companion.

The origins of the word *tiger* itself stem from a fantastic family of words that developed from the Indo-European root **STEIG-,** which means either "to stick" or "pointed." English *tiger* and its Greek predecessor, *tigris,* are thought to have come from dialects of Old Iranian, where *tighri-* means "arrow" and *tighra-* means "sharp," "pointed." Various explanations have been offered for this psychological link between tigers and arrows: the arrow-swift speed of a tiger's pounce, perhaps, or the sharpness of this animal's teeth, or its "arrow-shaped" stripes.

Indo-European **STEIG-** also poked its way into the Greek verb *stizein,* "to prick" or "tattoo," the source of *stigma,* "a mark made by piercing," and *astigmatism,* the medical condition in which the eye fails to focus on a "mark." In modern Greece, a *stigma* is a "moment" or "point" in time.

STEIG- also left its mark in the English word *instigate,* which literally means "to prod" or "spur on," and *stitch,* which one makes by piercing. This root's "piercing" sense is also reflected in its Old Norse derivative, *steikja,* "to roast (on a spit)," from which comes the English *steak.*

Another of this root's offspring is the Old French verb *estiquer,* which means "to stick" or "fix," and gave rise to English *ticket*—originally a note "affixed" or "stuck" on something. Both of these words are also closely related to the modern French word *etiquette.* By an etymological progression that isn't entirely clear, *etiquette* apparently evolved in meaning from "label" or "ticket" to "a prescribed routine," and eventually to the sense of "prescribed, mannerly behavior."

A final member of the word family that produced such "prickly" offspring as *ticket, tiger lily, steak,* and *stigma* is the splendid English word *snickersnee.* Once commonly used to mean either a kind of knife fighting or the knife used in such a contest, *snickersnee* is adapted from the Dutch phrase *steken en snijden,* literally, "to thrust and cut." (It is the *steken* in this phrase—and thus the *snick-* in *snickersnee*— that derives from Indo-European **STEIG-**.) The English term *snickersnee* is also spelled *snick and snee* or *snick-or-snee*—when it is spelled at all, that is. Any way you slice it though, *snickersnee*—you can almost hear the blades scraping against each other— is certainly another one of those delicious words that deserve to be revived.

Loosestrife

*I*f you ever need to extend a peace offering but can't find an olive branch, you can express the same sentiments with a sprig of yellow *loosestrife*. This flower's name is traditionally thought to refer to its purported power to "loosen" or ease "strife."

This belief, however, arose from a persistent bit of folk etymology. It is true that the Greeks' name for this flower, *lusimacheion,* derives from Greek *luein,* "to loosen," and *makhē,* "strife." But the real reason they called this plant *lusimacheion* is the fact that the fellow credited with discovering its real medicinal uses was name *Lusimakhos.* Nevertheless, claims about the soothing properties of loosestrife took root and multiplied. Pliny the Elder wrote that *lysimachia,* as the Romans called it, not only had the power to pacify angry beasts, but also repelled snakes, healed fresh wounds, and eased "sores caused by footwear." Lysimachia's therapeutic value was also extolled by Pliny's contemporary, the physician Dioscorides, whose writings were regarded as the Western world's chief authority on botany for nearly 1,700 years. A 1655 translation of Dioscorides notes that *lysimachia* "stays ye womanish flux & for ye issue of blood out of ye nostrils ye herb being stuft in is profitable."

. . .

THE LY- in the words *lusimacheion, Lusimakhos,* and *lysimachia* comes from the Indo-European root **LEU-1,** meaning "loosen," "divide," or "cut apart." From the same root comes English *loose, loosestrife,* and several other words worthy of note. From **LEU-1**'s Greek offspring *luein,* "loosen," comes the medical term *lysis,* which refers to either the gradual subsiding of acute symptoms or the destruction of cells. *Hemolysis* specifically denotes the breakdown of red blood cells (from Greek *haima,* "blood," the source of *hemorrhage* and *hemoglobin*). Added to the Greek stem *ana-,* meaning "back" or "again," *luein* formed the name of the "breaking into components" also known as *analysis.* When tacked on to Greek *para,* "to one side," *luein* formed the word for the "irregular loosening" (or "disabling," in other words) commonly called *paralysis.*

LEU-1 is represented in Latin by the verb *solvere,* "to loosen" or "to free," from which comes *absolve* ("to clear away") as well as *absolute* (literally "free from," and thus "complete"). Latin *solvere* is also in *dissolve* and *solve,* which is what one does to a knotty problem after it has "loosened."

Another Latin descendant of **LEU-1** is *lues,* meaning "plague" or "pestilence"—a disease that "dissolves" or "unbinds." This word was borrowed whole into English, where it is pronounced "Louie's" and denotes the disease more commonly called syphilis. (More about *syphilis* appears in the chapter on **Amaryllis**.)

Via the Germanic languages, **LEU-1** also made its way into such "loose" English derivatives as *lose, loss, lost,* the suffix *-less,* and *lorn,* meaning "lost" or "abandoned," as in *lovelorn* and *forlorn.* The English expression *forlorn hope,* which means "a hopeless or extremely difficult undertaking," also comes from this family, although its origin is not what you might expect. This phrase was first applied specifically as a military term, and referred to an advance guard of soldiers selected for an especially hazardous mission. *Forlorn hope* is adapted from the Dutch *verloren hoop,* or "lost troop," *verloren* being another descendant of **LEU-1,** and *hoop* being a word for "troop" or "company," and related to English *heap.* (A similar idea is reflected in the obsolete English word *perdue,* meaning "a soldier sent on a nearly hopeless mission." This word is from Old French *perdu,* "lost," and is kin to *perdition.*

THE origin of the *strife* in *loosestrife* is difficult to trace beyond its Old French counterpart, *estrif,* also kin to English *strive.* The source of the Greeks' word for "strife,"—the *makhē* in *Lusimakhos*—is likewise hard to determine. Greek *makhē* is, however, represented in a few other English words, most of which seem to be rather overwrought terms specifying various forms of conflict. A *logomachy,* from Greek

111

logos, "word," is a verbal battle about words. A *psychomachy* is a "conflict of the soul" or *psyche,* and a *tauromachy* is a "bullfight." *Sciamachy,* as you might recall from the chapter on **Anthurium,** is a lofty synonym for "shadow-boxing."

Some scholars say that *makhē*'s derivatives also include *Andromache,* the name of that most poignant character in Greek literature who has come to symbolize the suffering of women in wartime. Married to the Trojan hero Hector, Andromache saw her husband killed and mutilated and her infant son hurled from the walls of the city, and was herself taken captive. The stem *Andro-* comes from the Greek word for "man," and some translate her name as "she who does battle with men."

THE Latin word *Lysimachia,* by the way, now serves as the name of the scientific genus to which most loosestrife belongs. However, the flower popularly known as *purple loosestrife* belongs to an entirely different genus called *Lythrum,* the meaning of which couldn't be farther from that of "easing strife." The name *Lythrum,* which alludes to this plant's long spikes lined with deep red or purple blossoms, is the Latinized version of a Greek word that means "bloody gore."

Lupine

The *lupine* flower has long suffered a bad rap. Its name comes from Latin *lupus,* which means "wolf." The English adjective *lupine* describes someone or something "wolflike," or "ruthlessly predatory." The lupine flower is so named because of the way it thrives in poor soil—so well, in fact, that it gives the impression of "wolfing" nutrients out of the earth. Actually, just the opposite is true. Lupine is a nitrogen-fixing plant, which means that it increases soil fertility by converting nitrogen into a form that other plants can use.

The name *lupine* is applied loosely to several flowers, including the Texas bluebonnet, that are characterized by wandlike stalks of blossoms resembling the sweet pea. Lupine, also known as *wolf's bean,* belongs to the Pea family, or *Leguminosae,* and its seeds have been used as food since prehistoric times. In ancient Rome these seeds were used in the theater as stage "money," a practice that later prompted a seventeenth-century writer to observe, "As the Actors in Comedies paid all their Debts upon the Stage with Lupins, so a Sophist pays all his with Words." The lupine flower, accordingly, also goes by the name *penny bean.*

By taking a closer look at this flower maligned by

its own name, we'll meet a whole pack of lupine words, including *Lupercalia,* the strange fertility ritual that may have paved the way for our most romantic holiday, and *lycopodium,* a moss used in manufacturing products as diverse as fireworks and surgical gloves.

LUPINE

· · ·

To the ancients, wolves were the object of both fear and fascination. Latin *lupus* and its Greek counterpart, *lukos,* share a common ancestor, Indo-European **WLKWO-,** which also means "wolf." The reason **WLKWO-** looks so different from its Latin and Greek descendants is that both of these later wolf words arose from what are called "taboo variants" of the original root. Mindful of the magic power of the spoken word, our forebears substituted altered forms of certain words in order to avoid saying the name of something too dreadful to utter. Indo-European **WLKWO-** is more clearly seen in the names for the wolf in several other languages, including English and Dutch *wolf,* German *Wolf,* Lithuanian *vilkas,* Albanian *ul'k,* Old Prussian *wilkis,* and Sanskrit *vṛkas.*

Lupus and *lukos,* the Latin and Greek euphemisms for this beast of unspeakable ferocity, produced many offspring. Latin *lupus,* for example, was borrowed whole into English as the name of a disease that attacks the skin with peculiarly "wolflike" voraciousness. As a sixteenth-century medical text put it, "Lupus is a malignant ulcer quickly consum-

115

ing the neather [nether] part; and it is very hungry like unto a wolfe." The diminutive of Latin *lupus*, *lupulus*, inhabits the botanical name of the European hop plant, *Humulus lupulus*. The *Humulus* in its name apparently comes from an Old German word for "hop," and the "little wolf" reflects the way this twining vine tends to smother or "devour" the trees upon which it grows.

Lupus lurks within *lupanar*, a nineteenth-century English synonym for brothel, a loanword from the ancient Romans, who used the term *lupa* or "she-wolf" as a slang word for "prostitute." *Lupus* also left its tracks in English through its Spanish descendant, *lobo*, a loanword meaning "gray wolf" or "timberwolf."

One of the most fascinating descendants of Latin *lupus* is *Lupercalia*, the name of a festival held each February in ancient Rome. The curious rites of the Lupercalia most likely arose from extremely ancient ceremonies involving ritual purification and fertility enhancement. These rites began with the sacrifice of goats and a dog, after which a priest dabbed the animal's blood onto the foreheads of the two young men who had been selected for this honor. The priest then wiped away the blood with milk-soaked wool, at which point the two young men were, for some reason, expected to respond with a hearty laugh. Next the youthful pair ran around Rome clad in goatskin loincloths and thwacking everyone with strips of goat hide. This served as a form of ritual purification and was thought to increase fertility. This event provides the backdrop for Act I of Shakespeare's *Julius Caesar.* That year young Antony was elected to the youthful swat team, and Caesar advises his wife, Calphurnia, "Stand you directly in Antonio's way when he doth run his course," and reminds Antony, "Forget not . . . / To touch Calphurnia; for our elders say, / The barren, touched in this holy chase, / Shake off their sterile curse."

LUPINE
· · ·

So what's the connection between the Lupercalia and Latin *lupus*? There are at least two possible explanations, both of which have to do with wolves. The Romans themselves would answer that their Lupercalia stems from the worship of the gods Faunus and *Lupercus,* who shared the responsibility of protecting the Romans' herds and crops from such predators as wolves. However, it seems increasingly likely that the rites of the Lupercalia are vestiges of ceremonies from much earlier, pastoral societies— perhaps from the worship of *Lupa,* the legendary she-wolf who nursed Rome's eventual founders, or from the cult of the Goddess as Great She-Wolf, who was revered in prehistoric matrifocal societies.

Whatever its origins, the Lupercalia remained enormously popular for centuries until the early Christian church suppressed it, substituting in its place the Feast of the Purification of the Virgin Mary. Many historians also believe it was the mem-

ory of these pagan fertility rituals that the early church fathers were trying to erase by establishing a mid-February celebration of a Christian martyr— one who is recalled in modern times by believers and nonbelievers alike when they exchange tokens of affection on Valentine's Day.

By the way, those thongs toted by the Lupercalian runners were known as *februa,* a Latin word that means "instruments of purification." As a result, the name of the month in which these cleansing rituals took place was called *Februarius,* the source of English *February.* (Although the original sense of the word *February* may conjure some odd images, consider the alternative: We might have been stuck with the Anglo-Saxons' name for the year's second month, *solmōnath*—or literally, "Mud-Month."

THE ancient Greek cousin of Latin *lupus*—and thus a distant linguistic relative of the lupine flower—is *lukos,* a word found in a number of colorful Greek idioms. The ancient Greek word *lukospas,* or "torn by wolves," is a synonym for "bees," inspired by the ancient belief that these insects were generated inside the corpses of oxen ripped by wolves. *Lukophilia* was a bitter term for "treachery by a trusted friend"; literally, it means "wolf friendship." Plato's *Republic* includes the phrase *lukon idein,* which usually is watered down in English translations as "be astonished." In its most literal sense, however, the phrase means "to see a wolf"—an allusion to an old belief that anyone at whom a wolf got the first look would be struck speechless.

The Greeks' word for "wolf" also lurks inside several English words. From *lukos* and the Greek word *anthropos,* "human being," comes *lycanthropy,* which is usually defined as a form of insanity characterized by beastly behavior that is marked by a changed voice, depraved appetites, and generally lupine tendencies.

LUPINE

. . .

Lycopodium, or "wolf's foot," is the name of a moss whose roots bear a remarkable resemblance to a wolf's paw. (The Irish have a name for this moss that reflects a similar idea: *crúibíní sionnaig,* or "little feet of the fox.") The spores of lycopodium, also known as *vegetable brimstone* and *witches' meal,* form a fine, yellow powder that makes a dramatic flash when tossed into a flame. For this reason lycopodium was long used in the theater to create stage lightning and as an ingredient in fireworks. This water-repellent powder has also been used as a coating for pills and surgical gloves.

The *podium,* or "foot," in the name *lycopodium* is related to all those wonderful "foot" words from Indo-European **PED-1,** including Latin *pes,* "foot" (and its stem, *ped-,* as in *pedestrian* and *pedal*), as well as Greek *pous,* "foot" (and its stem *pod-,* as in *podiatrist*). The same root produced such cognates as French *pied,* Spanish *pie,* and Italian *piede* (the source of *piedmont,* "foothill country"), as well as English *foot* and its German cousin *Fuss,* as in *Fuss-*

ball.[1] The English word *podium* itself literally means "small foot," and refers to a platform or dais on which a speaker stands—not the lectern behind or beside which the speaker stands, as is often supposed.

Greek *lukos* also prowls around in the common vegetable garden. The botanical name of the tomato, *lycopersicum esculentum,* literally means "succulent wolf-peach." A less welcome "wolf" in one's garden is *lycoperdon,* otherwise known as the fungus puffball. The scientific term *lycoperdon* is actually a polite version of an antiquated English name for this fungus, *wolf's fist.* This particular *fist* isn't at all the same as a "clenched hand," however. In English the word *fist* was also once commonly used to mean what has been delicately defined as a "small windy escape backward," or as Samuel Johnson put it, "wind from behind." The verb *to fist,* by the way, is thought to be onomatopoetic.

To return to the *lycoperdon* or "wolf's fist," the *perdon* in its name comes from Greek *perdesthai,* "to break wind."[2] *Lycoperdon* is named for the fact that

· · · · · · · · · · · · · · · · · · · ·

[1] A little-known member of this family is the delightful word *piepowder.* It literally means "dusty-footed" (from Latin *pulvis,* "dust") and denotes "an itinerant merchant or wayfarer."

[2] This verb may also be the source of English *partridge.* Many scholars believe the name derives from the

when the puffball is split, it spews clouds of spores in a way reminiscent of the old-fashioned type of "fist." Over the years, this fungus was also called *puckfist* and *bullfist*.

IN addition to its ancient descendants, Latin *lupus* and Greek *lukos,* Indo-European **WLKWO-** is also responsible for the modern French word for "wolf," *loup*. French *loup* was borrowed by the English as the name of a type of velvet mask that women wore in the seventeenth century to protect their complexions. English speakers also adopted the French term *loup-garou,* which in both languages means "werewolf."

Loup is also found in some lively French idioms. *Entre chien et loup* means "twilight," although literally it translates as "between dog and wolf." This phrase is thought to refer either to the time of day when one can't distinguish between these animals at a distance, or to the notion of "being caught between" day and night. The French apparently inherited this idiom from the ancient Romans, who expressed the same idea with *inter canem et lupum.* The wolf plays a role in another French idiom, *tenir le loup par les oreilles,* "to hold a wolf by the ears" —a vivid means of describing the dilemma of being

• • • • • • • • • • • • • • • • • • • •

loud, whirring sound this bird makes when flushed from hiding.

trapped between holding on and letting go. Again, the Romans said it first, as *lupum auribus tenēre.* (The French also have a special fondness for the *loup,* however. *Mon loup,* or "my wolf," is a term of endearment, and *tête de loup,* or "wolf's head," is just "a long-handled feather duster.")

It may even be that there's a *loup* in the *Louvre.* Some etymologists think that the name of the world's largest museum stems from either the fact that the building stands in an area once frequented by wolves, or the fact that it was once the site of a hunting lodge where dogs and hawks were trained to hunt wolves.

FINALLY, the wolf also left the faintest of etymological footprints in the English word *tuxedo.* This word stems not from Greek or Latin, but ultimately from an indigenous language of the Americas. It seems that the western shore of the Hudson River was the home of a subtribe of the Delawares called the *P'tuksit,* which means "wolf-footed" or "round-footed." This was a name scornfully applied by others, suggesting that the *P'tuksit* were "easily toppled" in warfare—that these "round-footed" folk were, in other words, "pushovers."[3]

· · · · · · · · · · · · · · · · · · · ·

[3] Various languages of the Native Americans contain wonderfully creative and contemptuous names for "other folks." The state of *Iowa,* for example, is so called because

The English colonists who settled in P'tuksit territory anglicized the name of the Wolf Tribe to *Tucksito,* and eventually applied this name to that part of New York State. With a few linguistic alterations, *Tucksito* became *Tuxedo.* By the early nineteenth century this area had become *Tuxedo Park,* a wealthy resort town. In 1886 an heir to the Lorillard tobacco fortune caused a stir by attending the annual ball dressed in a formal dinner jacket minus the traditional tails. This new style quickly caught on and was named after the site of its debut.

LUPINE
. . .

Here's hoping that an equally innovative individual will one day make a fashion statement that acknowledges the *tuxedo*'s linguistic debt to the Native Americans—not to mention the wolves—who once roamed freely here. Perhaps some dapper visionary will start a new trend by removing the tuxedo's traditional boutonniere and replacing it with a sprig of that maligned and misunderstood blossom, the *lupine.*

. . . .

of a derogatory label applied to its Sioux inhabitants: *Ayuwha,* "the sleepy ones." The word *Apache* comes from a Zuni word for "enemy," and the name of the *Adirondacks* derives from the Mohawks' sneering epithet for that tribe, *Hatiróntaks,* or literally, "they eat trees."

Nasturtium

*W*ant to give someone's nose a playful tweak? Then send some *nasturtiums,* whose name derives from Latin *nasus,* "nose," and *torquere,* "to twist," because of their peppery, "nose-twisting" taste. With bright blossoms that range from yellow or deep orange to red, nasturtiums make a colorful, spicy addition to green salads.

As we consider the linguistic roots of the nasturtium, we'll investigate a number of "nose" words in several languages, including English *nose nippers, narks,* and *nosewings.* We'll also turn our attention to such "twisted" words as *tort, torture,* and *extortion.* Finally, we'll visit an austere order of monks, some rather bluenosed brethren who, in a wonderfully twisted way, share a common linguistic heritage not only with the Italian and French words for "nasturtium," but also with, of all things, a steaming cup of *cappuccino.*

THE *nas-* in *nasturtium,* as well as the English word *nose,* arose from an Indo-European root called **NAS-,** meaning "nose." The same root also protrudes from the names for noses in several languages, such as German *Nase,* Russian *nos,* Lithuanian *nósis,* and, as noted before, Latin *nasus.* (A form of Latin

nasus, by the way, is also part of the full name of the Roman poet widely considered the finest of his generation, Publius Ovidius *Naso,* otherwise known as Ovid. His family's last name means "large-nosed.") Latin *nasus* also gave rise to the English words *nasal* and *nasute,* the latter of which applies to anyone who has a particularly noticeable *nasus.* There's a whiff of Indo-European **NAS-** in the Latin word *naris,* or "nostril," as well. From Latin *naris* came the English word *nares* and the word for "nose" in both Spanish and Portuguese, *nariz.*

Via the Germanic language family, Indo-European **NAS-** also traveled into English, where it now resides in such words as *nozzle, nuzzle,* and *ness* ("a promontory" or "headland"). The same root also poked its way into an old Gypsy word for "nose," *nāk,* which later produced the English slang word *nark,* meaning "spy," "informer"—a "nose," in other words.

NAS- also made its way into English through the French loanword *pince-nez,* the name of those eyeglasses that "pinch" the nose—and which are also known as *nose nippers.* Similarly, French *nez percé,* or "pierced nose," entered the English language as the name applied to certain Native Americans in the Pacific Northwest, after French explorers reported seeing them wearing seashells in their noses.

Speaking of piercing, if your recipient is *thrilled* with a nosegay of nasturtiums, then he or she is literally "pierced through" with delight, because *thrill* is a variant of Old English *thyrel,* meaning a "hole" or a "boring-through." Old English *thyrel* comes from the Indo-European root **TERƏ-,** meaning "cross over" or "pass through." The same root is the source of such words as *through, thorough,* and *eye-thurl,* the last of which is an archaic word for "window"—a *window* being literally, as we saw in the chapter on **Daisy,** a "wind-eye." Indo-European **TERƏ-** is also found in the Old English word *nos-thyrl,* or "nose-hole," which, like the pungent nasturtium leaf, cleared the way for our *nostrils.*

NASTURTIUM

• • •

THE English word *nose* is also part of the picturesque term *nosewing,* which dictionaries say denotes "the arch of cartilage on either side of the nose." Thomas Wolfe once wrote about someone who "laughed . . . slyly, rubbing her nosewing with a finger." In anatomical textbooks this structure is called an *ala,* which means basically the same thing, as it comes from Latin *ala,* "wing," the source also of English *aisle* (via Old French *aile,* "a building's 'wing' "), and *alary,* an English word for "winglike."

A similar idea is found in the German word for "nostril," which is a real mouthful: In Germany, one rubs one's *Nasenflügel.* (German *Flügel,* or "wing," by the way, now resides in two musical English words: The *flugelhorn* was once used to summon an army's flanks or "wings," and a *flugel* is a grand piano, so named for its "winglike" contours.)

Contrary to appearances, *nosism* is not what one

127

might expect. This archaic English word has nothing to do with noses. It comes from the Latin word *nos*, or "we," and is defined as "the habit of using the word *we* when offering one's opinions," or "the arrogance or pride of a group of persons." *Nosism* is kin to such "we" words as Spanish *nos* and French *nous*, as well as English *nostrum*, literally, "our own" secret remedy.

SPEAKING of noses, the ancient Greek word *muxa* could mean either "nasal mucus" or "lampwick." This connection isn't all that farfetched when you consider the similar appearance of a wick sticking out of an oil lamp's nozzle and a string of mucus from a nostril. (Similarly, French *moucher* can mean either "snuff out a candle" or "blow one's nose," as in the handy expression *mouche ton nez!,* or "blow your own nose!" French *moucher* is kin to such words as Italian *mocciacaglia*—either "snail slime" or "snot"—English *mucus,* and the lovely but rarely used English word for "handkerchief," *muckender.*)

Greek *muxa* also oozed through the Romance languages and into a common English word. By a marvelous series of etymological twists and turns, the linguistic descendants of *muxa* evolved in meaning from "the cord that burns in an oil lamp," to "the wick that is lit when firing a musket," and eventually to the name of that familiar igniting device we call a *match.*

• • •

LET us now turn our attention to the -*turtium* or "twisting" in *nasturtium*. Its Latin source, *torquere*, "to twist," comes from the Indo-European root **TERKW-,** which means the same thing. From this root also comes English *torch* (originally made from "twisted" fibers or twigs) *torture* (a "twisting" or "writhing"), and *torque* (a "twisting, turning force" or "a bracelet or collar made by twisting").[1]

NASTURTIUM

• • •

The -*turtium,* in *nasturtium* is also kin to the legal term *tort,* which means a "wrongful act"—a bad "turn," in other words. Torts often lead to civil suits in which one party accuses the other of *distorting* or "twisting" the facts, prompting the accused to "turn back" such claims with *retorts,* or perhaps even even allegations of *extortion,* or "wringing out"—all of which leads to still more legal *contortions* of one kind or another, with the result that the whole process becomes *tortuous,* or "twisted and convoluted," not to mention *torturous,* so that eventually everybody winds up feeling bent out of shape.

The same "twist" in English *tort* appears in other languages' words about "wrongs." The Italian expression *aver torto* means "to be wrong." The same is true of French *avoir tort,* which is found in

• •

[1] The word *collar,* by the way, is from Latin *collum,* "neck," also found in *décolletage,* a "low-cut neckline," as well as *decollation,* for which the guillotine was invented, and *torticollis,* the medical abnormality of having a "twisted neck."

the wise and wry proverb *Les absents ont toujours tort:* "Those absent are always wrong," since they can't be there to defend themselves. Even the English word *wrong* evokes the idea of "crooked" or "twisted"; it comes from another Indo-European root that means "to turn or bend." (This root, **WER-3,** produced several other wayward words, including *wrangle, wring, wrinkle,* and *worry,* the last of which once carried a far more vivid sense of "strangling" or "throttling," before it became diluted in meaning.)

To turn once again to the nose-twisting nasturtium: The French call this flower a *capucine,* and the Italians, a *cappuccina.* Both names are linguistically related to the name of the drink made with espresso and hot milk, *cappuccino*—and in a way that is deliciously roundabout.

The Italian word for "nasturtium," *cappuccina,* comes from the Italian word for "hood" or "cowl," *cappuccio.* This is because part of the nasturtium blossom resembles a little pointed hood. The nasturtium's French name, *capucine,* is adapted from the Italian. These words are descendants of Latin *caput,* "head," and kin to such English words as *cape, cap, capital, captain,* and *chief,* as well as *achieve* (literally, "to come to a head"), *mischief* ("to come to a head in a bad way"), and *kerchief* (a "covering for the head").

Capucine was borrowed into English as a synonym for "nasturtium." The same word is found in the expression *capucine capers,* once commonly used to denote "the pickled seeds of a nasturtium," as well as another nickname for the nasturtium plant itself. Similarly, the German name for the nasturtium is *Kapuzinerkresse,* the word *Kresse* being a cognate of English *cress,* a name applied to several plants that have a peppery flavor.

NASTURTIUM

· · ·

To see the linguistic link between nasturtiums and cappuccino, one must first consider the strict monastic order known as the *Capuchins.* These monks were so famous for their public displays of religious devotion that they inspired words in several languages, and not all of them complimentary. A *capuchinade,* according to one French dictionary, is a *tirade moralisante plate et banale,* that is, a "dull and hackneyed moralizing tirade."

These pious folk were also well known for their plain garb consisting of a single cloak topped with a pointy hood. The Franciscan monk who founded the Capuchin order did so after becoming convinced that the Franciscan habit was not an authentic version of the one that St. Francis had worn. This monk argued his case so zealously that at last the Pope granted him permission to form a separate monastic order that would minister to the poor and wear authentic habits with their distinctive pointed hoods.

The Capuchins, then, like the nasturtiums of Italy and France, take their names from the Italian for "hood." As a loanword in English, *capuchin* has also

come to mean "a woman's hooded cape," and "a South American monkey that has a bald forehead and black hair resembling a cowl," and "a pigeon with feathers on its head that resemble a hood."

What, then, is the linguistic tie that binds monks, nasturtiums, and a cup of cappuccino? The answer is that the name of the drink was inspired by the drab color of a Capuchin's cloak. Incidentally, the Capuchins weren't the only monks to bequeath their name to a beverage. The *Carthusian* monks of France also became well known for the bright yellow-green liqueur they manufactured. This drink's name, as well as its color, commemorates its monastic makers: The word *Carthusian* is a Latinized version of the name of the village high in the French Alps where this order was founded—a place called *Chartreuse.*

Orchid

*T*hat most elegant of flowers, the *orchid,* is named not for its alluring blossom but for its twin bulbs that bear a rather unnerving resemblance to testicles. Its name derives from the ancient Greek word *orkhis,* which means "testicle." Thus the name of the orchid is related to such words as *orchitis,* or "inflammation of a testicle," as well as *cryptorchidism,* the condition of having an undescended or "hidden" testicle, and *orchiectomy,* a surgical procedure for which, one suspects, few men would readily volunteer.

The origin of the Greek word *orkhis* itself is difficult to determine. It is thought to come from the Indo-European root **ERGH-,** which means "to mount." Some scholars link *orchis* and **ERGH-** to the Greek word *orkhein,* which means "to dance," the source of English *orchestra*—the *orchestra* in an ancient Greek theater being the area where the chorus danced.[1] Orchids belong to a huge botanical family, the *Orchidaceae,* or Orchid family. A closer look at orchids and their many nicknames will lead

· · · · · · · · · · · · · · · · · · · ·

[1] Incidentally, in *A Dictionary of Slang and Unconventional English,* Eric Partridge points out that *orchestra stalls* and its shortened form, *orks,* are both colloquial terms for "testicles," formed by rhyming slang on the word *balls.*

us to a discussion of, among other things, some alleged aphrodisiacs, including the delicious fruit that gets its name from the Aztecs' word for "testicle." We'll also meet a few other botanical wonders, some of them quite familiar, that are named for their resemblance to sex organs, both male and female.

ORCHID

· · ·

THE uncanny resemblance between an orchid bulb and male gonads seems to have encouraged the belief that orchids possess extraordinary aphrodisiac powers. Pliny the Elder wrote of the Greeks' belief that merely holding an orchid bulb in one's hand would arouse sexual desire, and that a potion of orchid roots mixed with dry wine was even more potent. This drink was also supposed to work wonders for rams and billy goats that were considered "too sluggish."

Over the centuries, the orchid's romantic reputation inspired quite a few earthy nicknames. In English this flower is sometimes called a *satyrion,* a name also used in ancient Greece and Rome. Roman legend had it that the satyrion was so named because it sprang from semen spilled by those lusty mythical creatures, the *satyrs,* who also inspired the term *satyriasis,* the male version of nymphomania.

In France, an orchid is sometimes called a *testicule de prêtre,* or "priest's testicles." In Germany, this flower is sometimes known as a *Knabenkraut,* or "boy plant"—*Knabe* being kin to English *knave,* and *Kraut* being a generic term that means "plant."

Several graphic English nicknames for orchids arise from the once-common use of *stone* as a synonym for "testicle." This also occurs in Danish and Swedish, where *sten* means either "stone" or "testicle." One type of orchid, for example, goes by the English nicknames *fool's stones* and *fool's ballocks*. (The same idea is reflected in that orchid's scientific name, *Orchis morio*. In Latin, *morio* means "stupid person," and gave rise to English *moron* and *oxymoron*, a "pointedly foolish" assertion, from the Greek *oxus*, "sharp.")

Other vivid names for the orchid assign ownership of its distinctive bulbs to various animals. These less-than-romantic flower names include *goatstones, dogstones*, and *foxstones*. A sixteenth-century English herbal listed another: "Whyt satyrion . . . or in other more unmanerly speche, *hares ballockes* [*hare's ballocks*]." The comparison of orchid bulbs to *foxstones*, by the way, is also preserved within the English loanword *salep*, a borrowing from a Turkish name for this food similar to tapioca made by drying and grinding certain orchid bulbs. Turkish *salep*, in turn, is adapted from the Arabic *khasyu ath-tha'lab*, which literally means "the fox's testicles."

STILL another startling English name for the orchid blossom is *sweet cods*. As you may have guessed, the word *cods* is yet another term for "testicle" or "scrotum." It's the same *cod*, in fact, as in the cod-covering piece of apparel called a *cod-*

piece, and is kin to Swedish *kudde,* "cushion" or "pillow."

ORCHID

• • •

Orchids sometimes go by the name *soldier's cullions.* The word *cullions,* yet another antiquated English term for "testicles," is kin to Spanish *cojones.* Both *cullions* and *cojones* descended, so to speak, from a Greek word for "sheath," *koleos*—a word which also inspired the name of the familiar houseplant, *coleus,* the stamens of which are enclosed in a sheath.

Also related to *cullions, cojones,* and *coleus* is the scientific name *coleoptera,* which applies to beetles and other insects having a pair of hard wings that "sheathe" the more delicate wings used for flight. (The *-ptera* in *coleoptera,* by the way, comes from Greek *pteron,* meaning "wing," the source of such winged words as *feather* and the aircraft with "spiraling" or "helical" wings, a *helicopter.* Add the Greek prefix *a-,* "not," and you get the name of the bird in the "B.C." comic strip that always says, "Hi there. I am an *apteryx,* a wingless bird with hairy feathers.")

Before leaving Greek *koleos* entirely, we should recall that the Latin word for "sheath" is *vagina.* From Latin *vagina* came the Spanish word for "sheath," *vaina*—and from that word's diminutive, *vainilla,* comes the name of the *vanilla plant,* which is distiguished by its long, aromatic seed pods or "sheaths." The *vanilla plant,* by the way, also happens to be a member of the Orchid family.

(And as long as we're giving equal time to plants with names containing female sexual imagery, we should note that the flower commonly known as the *butterfly pea* belongs to the scientific genus called *Clitoria,* so named, as *Webster's* obliquely puts it, "from the appearance of the flower.")

THE etymological roots of the orchid and the vanilla bean may come as a surprise, but our linguistic for-bears just weren't bashful about calling things as they saw them. In fact, orchids aren't the only familiar plants named after testicles.

The Aztecs applied their word for "testicle," *ahu-acatl,* to an exquisite green fruit with a similar shape. This word was among the many things Spanish con-quistadors took from the indigenous peoples of Mexico and Central America. The word *ahuacatl* be-came more comfortable on the Spanish tongue as *avocado,* a word that was transplanted whole into English as the name of the fleshy, testicle-shaped fruit. In the same way, with their word for "sauce," *molli,* the Aztecs formed their name for the greenish mishmash they called *ahuacamolli*—which the Span-iards tasted and pronounced *guacamole.* In modern Mexico, *mole* is a spicy sauce made from chile, choc-olate, and other ingredients.

The avocado, like the orchid, was long considered an aphrodisiac. Louis XIV of France was reportedly so impressed with this fruit's power to excite sexual passion that he referred to it as *la bonne poire,* or "the good pear." (Then again, maybe he used this phrase to avoid confusion: The French word *avocat* can mean either "avocado" or "lawyer"—the result of two distinct etymological progressions that led to different words spelled exactly alike.[2] French *avocat,* when it refers to the fruit, is adapted from Spanish *avocado.* French *avocat,* in the legal sense, is a cognate of English *advocate,* both of these words coming from Latin *advocatus,* "someone called or summoned.")

ORCHID

• • •

It is appropriate to conclude by mentioning that the words *advocate* and *advocatus,* as well as the lawyerly French *avocat,* are kin to a wonderful name for a type of eggnog noted for its usefulness in soothing the throats of those inclined to long-windedness. The drink is called *advocaat,* a word borrowed directly into English from the Dutch. A cup of advocaat contains eggs, sugar, brandy, coffee flavoring, and vanilla (but no avocados).

So why is this drink called advocaat? This name is

• • • • • • • • • • • • • • • • • •

---

[2] Another example of two different linguistic progressions leading to words spelled exactly alike is English *cleave,* which appears to mean the opposite of itself. The word *cleave,* meaning "adhere to," as in the biblical "cleave to his wife," comes from Old English *cleofian,* "to stick to," and is related to such "sticky" words as *clammy* and *clench.* However, *cleave* can also mean "to split from" as in *meat cleaver, cloven,* and *cleft.* This *cleave* comes from Old English *clēofan,* "split, cut."

actually a shortened form of the Dutch *advocatenborrel,* which means "advocate drink"—a name that celebrates, according to *Webster's,* this concoction's "throat-soothing effect, especially helpful for irritations caused by the traditional eloquence of lawyers."

Pansy

"And there is pansies, that's for thoughts..."
—Ophelia, *Hamlet,* IV, v.

*T*he name *pansy* came from the French word for "thought," *pensée.* This blossom is named for the way it resembles a little face frowning as if deep in contemplation. French *pensée* and English *pansy* belong to a whole brood of thoughtful, weighty words, including *pensive, ponder,* and *ponderous.*

The pedigree of these words stretches all the way back to an Indo-European root designated as **(S)PEN-,** "to draw, stretch, or spin." From this source came such "spinning" words as the German *Spinne,* or "spider," and its Old English cousin, *spī-thra,* which later became English *spider.* To see how **(S)PEN-** eventually gave rise to such "thinking" words as *pansy,* it is first necessary to understand some of its other offspring.

This root's ancient sense of "drawing" or "stretching" in turn led to several words related to the idea of "hanging." **(S)PEN-** is represented, for example, in Latin *pendēre,* "to cause to hang," which gave us English *pendulum* and *pendant,* as well as the adjective *pendent,* which describes pendulums, pendants, or anything else that is "hanging." When something is hanging in a metaphorical sense, it is said to be *pending,* just as something "hanging overhead"—that is, menacingly—is said to be *impending.*

Other "hanging" descendants of Indo-European **(S)PEN-** include *perpendicular,* from Latin *perpendiculum,* or "plumbline," and *pensile,* pronounced like "pencil," which means "hanging from above." (For the origin of *pencil,* see the chapter on **Anthurium**.)

To *depend,* in a literal sense, is "to hang down" from something else. To *suspend* is to "hang up from underneath" (from Latin *sub-,* "under")—to interrupt something, or leave it "hanging," in other words. Television producers often attempt to create *suspense* with a "cliffhanger," although such episodes often require audiences to *suspend* disbelief.

Something that is *appended* is "hung on" or attached, such as the *appendix* to a book. One's own appendix (technically called the *vermiform,* or "worm-shaped," *appendix*) hangs from the blind pouch at the beginning of the large intestine. (In case you were wondering, *Webster's* points out that *appendix* is also the name for "the tube that is located at the bottom of a balloon and is used in inflation and deflation.") *Append* and *appendix* are also related to the name for the apartment on the top floor of a building, the *penthouse.* This word was formed by folk etymology, by an alteration of Middle English *pentis,* from Old French *appentis,* which derives

in turn from Medieval Latin *appendicium,* literally "something hung on."

ANOTHER Latin derivative of **(S)PEN-**—and a very close relative of Latin *pendēre,* "to hang"—is *pendere,* "to weigh." The close connection between these two Latin words reflects the fact that in antiquity weighing was accomplished by balancing items on a set of hanging scales. This image of "weighing," and thus of "weighing out"—or "paying," in other words—is evident in several modern words. When the Latin preposition *ex,* or "out," was appended to *pendere,* the result was *expendere,* "to weigh out," "pay out," which led to English *expend* and *expense.* These "paying" words are also related to *spend* and *dispense,* as well as the proper names *Spenser* and *Spencer,* literally, "a dispenser of goods."

Similarly, when the Romans added their stem *com-,* "together," to a form of their word for "weigh," *pensare,* the result was *compensare,* the forerunner of English *compensate*—literally, to "weigh together," or "counterbalance" one thing with something else of equal value. Compensation sometimes comes in the form of a *pension,* money "paid out" or "dispensed" to retired employees. In some countries such compensation may be paid in *pesos,* a word that happens to be another member of this "weighing," "paying" family: In Spanish, *peso* literally means "weight."

This family also includes *avoirdupois,* from Old

French *aver de peis,* "goods or property of weight" —the *aver* meaning "property" (akin to English *have*)—and the *peis* coming from Latin *pendere,* "weigh." The latter part of *avoirdupois* is a cousin of English *poise,* a word that calls to mind the image of ancient scales when they have reached the point of "balance" or "equilibrium." *To poise* is literally to be "in suspension" or "still in a state of balance"— at least for that particular instant in time.

PANSY

. . .

Other weighty descendants of **(S)PEN-** include Latin *pondo,* or "weight," from which comes the English unit of measure, *pound,* and *preponderate,* literally, "to exceed in weight." There's also English *ponderous,* or "heavy," and the name of the tall, heavy pine tree found throughout the western United States, the *ponderosa.*

All of this is something to *ponder,* which is, of course, what you do when you weigh something mentally. Thus the primitive sense of Indo-European **(S)PEN-** extended through words that refer to "drawing" or "stretching" to others involving "hanging" and "weighing," eventually to the abstract idea of "thinking." Other "thoughtful" descendants of Latin *pendere,* or "weigh," include English *pensive,* which means "thoughtful," and Spanish *pensamiento,* "thought." In fact, like French *pensée,* the Spanish word *pensamiento* not only means "thought" or "mind," but also serves as the name for the pansy.

. . .

THE pansy goes by an unusually large number of nicknames. The appearance of its blossom has inspired such names as *flower-with-a-face,* and *three-faces-under-a-hood.* Because this blossom is usually marked with three different colors, it also goes by the name *herb trinity.*

Pansies are also known by such idyllic names as *love-in-idleness* and *heartsease,* the latter being an English synonym for "tranquility." Other nicknames suggest that the pansy has long been associated with matters of the heart: *Cupid's delight, St. Valentine's flower, kiss-me-at-the-garden-gate, kiss-me-quickly, Johnny-jump-up, jump-up-and-kiss-me,* and plain old *kiss-me.*

Perhaps the most picturesque of all the pansy's names, however, is the standard German word for this flower, *Stiefmütterchen.* While speakers of English and French see in the pansy's face a thoughtful frown, Germans see the unforgiving scowl of a "little stepmother." In fact, words from several languages betray an especially nasty attitude toward stepmothers. The ancient Romans, for example, called a "stepmother" a *noverca* (literally, "the new one," as in *novice, novelty,* and *renovate*), which led to the Latin adjective *novercalis,* meaning "hostile" or "malevolent." It was considered particularly unpleasant to be glared at with *oculibus novercalibus* or "stepmother eyes." English *novercal,* meaning "of or like a stepmother," also carries a derogatory sense; Robert Browning once described someone as being "of true novercal type, dragon and devil."

Italians now apply the word *matrigna,* or "stepmother," to anyone or anything "cruel," "hostile," or "contrary." The diplomatic French came up with two expressions for "stepmother": *Belle mère,* literally, "beautiful mother," can mean either "stepmother" or "mother-in-law," and *marâtre,* specified in French-English dictionaries as "[cruel] stepmother." Today *marâtre* is even used as a technical term in metallurgy to mean "the hottest part of a furnace."

PANSY

· · ·

THE word *pansy* inevitably calls to mind its use as a slang term for "male homosexual" or "effeminate man." Just how this came about is unclear. Eric Partridge's *Dictionary of Slang and Unconventional English* notes that the word *daisy* has been used in the same way since the 1950s. Partridge suggests that *pansy* may have come to mean "male homosexual" because of its rhyme with *Nancy,* which, along with *Nancy boy* and *Miss Nancy,* has been around for a while as a slang term for "catamite," that is, "a boy kept by a pederast." (*Catamite,* by the way, comes from *Ganymede,* the name of a comely Trojan boy whom Zeus carried off to serve as his personal cupbearer.)

In *Another Mother Tongue,* author Judy Grahn offers another possible explanation. She suggests

that the connection between pansies and gay men may have its origins in the sixteenth century, when men and women signaled their intent never to marry by wearing a sprig of violets—the color of which is traditionally associated with the gay community.

The pansy itself is, after all, simply a cultivated variety of violet. Its scientific name, *Viola tricolor,* means "three-color violet." The Latin flower name *viola* (no relation to the musical instrument) and its English offspring, *violet,* stem from the non–Indo-European source that also produced the Greek word for "violet," *ion.* (From this Greek flower name comes English *iodine,* the chemical element named for the violet-covered vapor it produces.) The intimate relationship between the cultivated pansy and the wild violet is nowhere more evident than in the Italian name for the pansy. It also reflects what Ophelia knew, even in her madness—for the Italians call this flower *la viola del pensiero,* "the violet of thought."

Poppy

*T*he gently nodding *poppy* has long been associated with sleep, dreams, and numbing relief. "Nature," wrote Emerson, "wherever she mars her creature . . . lays her poppies plentifully on the bruise." In *The Wizard of Oz,* Dorothy and her pals nearly lose their way when they come across some poppies whose narcotic properties have been magically enhanced. This link between poppies and dreamy anesthesia arises from the fact that one type of poppy is the source of opium. In German, this poppy goes by the more literal name *Schlafmohn,* or "sleep-poppy," and in Spanish it is called the *adormidera*—a linguistic cousin of such "sleepy" English words as *dormant* and *dormitory.*

Ancient Egyptians adorned their mummified princesses with poppies to ensure their pleasant dreams in the afterlife. In Greek myth, the earth goddess, Demeter, became so distraught in her ceaseless search for her kidnapped daughter Persephone that the other gods felt sorry for her and commanded poppies to spring up in her path; when she stopped to pick one she fell into a deep sleep. The poppy was also sacred to Demeter's Roman counterpart, Ceres, the goddess who presided over agriculture, especially the growth of grain. (From her name comes our own word *cereal*.) Poppies often grow wild among cultivated crops, and indeed in parts of England the poppy is still known as the *corn rose*.

POPPY

• • •

In many traditions poppies are thought to grow from the blood of those who have been slain. After World War I so many poppies bloomed throughout the battlefields of Europe that many nations, including the United States, decided to honor those who were killed there by designating the period leading up to Memorial Day as *Poppy Week.*

THE earliest origins of the poppy's name are unclear. It is known that the Romans called this blossom *papaver,* the source of this flower's English name. Because some poppies proved to be useful bleaching agents, the Romans applied the Latin adjective *papaveratus* to any toga that was "made shining white with poppies." The image of these dazzling garments, by the way, is preserved within the English word *candidate*. (More about this practice in the chapter on **Lily**.)

Latin *papaver,* or "poppy," also produced counterparts of the English word *poppy* in several languages, such as French *pavot* and Italian *papavero*. In Italy an *alto papavero* is a "prominent person" or "bigwig," although the expression literally means "a tall poppy"—which of course gives a whole new meaning to the nickname of President George "Poppy" Bush.

The Latin word *papaver* remains with us in one

other English word, *papaverine,* the name of a drug made from poppies. Recent scientific research suggests that certain types of male sexual impotence may be alleviated with a strategically placed injection of papaverine.

Some other languages use names for the poppy which derive from an entirely different ancient source, **MAK-1,** which means "poppy." This root seems to have been borrowed from a tongue spoken by a pre-Indo-European people living near the Mediterranean. From **MAK-1** comes the name of the poppy in German, *Mohn,* and Russian *mak.* A trace of this root also shows up in English *maw seed,* the name of a type of poppy seed used in bird food.

MAK-1 also produced the ancient Greek word for "poppy," *mēkōn.* Here our discussion turns unsavory: You can credit—or blame—the Greeks for noticing that the dark juice from poppies, a liquid they call *mēkōnion,* looked an awful lot like a baby's first feces. They found this resemblance so striking, in fact, that they started using the same word, *mēkōnion,* to denote either substance. From this curious connection also comes the modern English term for that first diaperful, *meconium.*

IF the thought of a connection between poppies and baby poop sounds like so much poppycock—well, that's exactly what it is, in a manner of speaking. This is because the *poppy* in *poppycock* has nothing to do with flowers. It comes instead from Dutch *pappekak,* or literally, "soft shit." English speakers who heard this useful Dutch expression corrupted it into a form that sounded more familiar to them, and this once graphic word has since become a rather colorless euphemism for much stronger language.

POPPY

. . .

While we're on the subject of *poppycock,* let us veer from our discussion of poppies proper, and venture instead onto another slippery but most instructive etymological path—for a brief look at the roots of this word. The source of the first part of Dutch *pappekak* (and thus English *poppycock*) is the Indo-European root **PAP-2,** meaning "food." This root also produced English *pap,* which originally meant "soft, pulpy food for babies" and has since come to mean "tedious, mindless entertainment," and also "political patronage." (A *Pap* test, however, is named for the scientist who invented it, George Papanicolaou.)

The Indo-European root **PAP-2** also appears to have produced English *pamper,* originally "to cram with food." This word later developed the more abstract sense of "to spoil" or "to baby" someone. And in a wonderfully roundabout way, the more primitive sense of *pamper*—that of "cramming with food"— would seem to make this word doubly appropriate as the brand name for a disposable diaper.

Having disposed of the first part of *pappekak* and *poppycock,* let us turn to the latter portions of these words. Dutch *kak,* or "shit," comes from another Indo-European root that scholars have recon-

153

structed as **KAKKA-,** meaning "to defecate." Some authorities describe this root as "imitative" in origin.

KAKKA- made its way into Latin, where it inspired the verb *cacare,* "to defecate." From Latin *cacare* came several English words, now obsolete, including *cuck,* "to defecate," and *cuckingstool,* literally, "defecating chair," which was applied to an instrument of torture used in early medieval England to punish those citizens judged to be a public nuisance. The cuckingstool consisted of a chamberpot chair attached to the end of a long plank. The victim was tied to the chair and ridiculed, and sometimes ducked in a pond. Just which members of the population were most likely to suffer such punishment is obvious from the definition for this device in Samuel Johnson's 1755 *Dictionary:* "An engine invented for the punishment of scolds and unquiet women . . ."

Another relative of *cuck* and *cuckingstool* is *cack,* which means either "to defecate" or "to vomit." As a noun, *cack* can mean "dung," or "muck."

KAKKA- found its way into ancient Greek, where it produced *kakos,* or "bad," now found in such English words as *cacophony,* or "bad sound," and *cacophonophilist,* someone who delights therein. A person who is *cacophrenic* is "of inferior intellect." *Cacography* can mean either "bad handwriting" or "bad spelling." *Kakos,* when added to the Greek word *ethos,* or "habit," formed the useful but little-used English word *cacoethes,* which means "habitual, uncontrollable desire." The Latin phrase *cacoethes*

POPPY

. . .

scribendi is still found in English dictionaries, where it is defined as "an uncontrollable urge to write."

KAKKA- is reflected in some English word borrowings from other languages as well. The Spanish word *cacafuego* is usually defined as "a braggart" or "spitfire," but its literal meaning is "shit-fire." This expression became somewhat popular in England after Sir Francis Drake captured a ship of the same name.[1] Likewise, the name for an apple once popular in England, the *coccagee,* is adapted from the Irish expression *cac a' ghéidh,* literally, "dung of goose," a name inspired by the greenish-yellow color of both.

The same word family that produced *cuck, cack, cacafuego,* and the *-cock* in *poppycock* also gave rise to a Yiddish expression for another disagreeable type of person, *alter kocker,* the polite translation of which is something like "old fogey." This expression and its abbreviated form, *A.K.,* enjoyed wide usage in this country in the 1930s.

Finally, at the risk of appearing to have a *cacoethes scribendi* concerning **KAKKA-,** I'd like to note one last descendant from this prolific root: *Korinthenkacker.* German *Korinthe* means "raisin" or "currant." (The word *Korinthe,* like its English cousin *currant,* stems from the fact that this wrinkled fruit

. . . .

[1] Spanish *fuego,* or "fire," by the way, is related to such "fiery" English words as *focus,* from Latin *focus,* or "hearth," and *curfew,* from Old French *cuevrefeu,* "a covering of the fire."

was once exported primarily from the Greek port city of *Corinth*.) Usually applied to small-time bureaucrats, the German word *Korinthenkacker* is an exquisitely appropriate term. Literally, it means "raisin-crapper."

Rose

*B*y any other name, of course, this blossom would smell as sweet, but in several Indo-European languages, the names for the rose are remarkably similar. In French, German, Danish, and Norwegian a rose is a *rose.* In Italian, Spanish, and Portuguese the rose is a *rosa.* The Dutch call this flower a *roos,* the Irish a *ros,* the Welsh a *rhosyn,* and the Russians and Bulgarians refer to it as a *roza.*

In each of these languages, "rose" comes from an extremely ancient root that scholars have reconstructed as **WROD-,** which may have been borrowed from a still older Mediterranean tongue. Vestiges of this root are visible in the modern Armenian word for "rose," *vard,* and in Old English *word,* meaning "thornbush."

WROD- is also reflected in the early Greeks' word for "rose," *wrodon.* Eventually this word lost its initial *w,* becoming *rhodon* in classical Greek.[1] In the *Odyssey,* for example, Homer is forever mention-

. . . .

[1] In modern Greece, the rose often goes by an entirely different, but picturesque name. There a rose is called a *triantaphyllo,* or "the flower of thirty petals." This name is also related to the Romanians' word for "rose," *trindafir,* and the Albanians' *trendafil.*

ing *rhododactulos Ēōs,* or "rosy-fingered Dawn."
Traces of Greek *rhodon* are evident in several modern English words as well. The chemical element *rhodium,* or *Rh,* is a silvery white metal named for the "rose red" color of its compounds. *Rhodium wood* is the "rose-scented" wood of shrubs native to the island of Tenerife.

ROSE

· · ·

The Greek isle of *Rhodes,* off the coast of Turkey, is also thought to have derived its name from the ancient Greek word for "rose." This name may refer to the abundance of roses on that island, or to the fact that the rose was the special flower of the sun god, Helios, to whom this island was sacred. Some scholars make the intriguing suggestion that the isle of Rhodes went by a similar-sounding name in the language of its much earlier pre–Indo-European inhabitants, and that the island's association with roses in later years provided the Greeks with a convenient excuse for a little folk etymology.

(The island of Rhodes was also famous for its gigantic bronze statue of Helios. According to various classical accounts it towered as high as 120 feet above the island's harbor. The Colossus of Rhodes was considered one of the Seven Wonders of the Ancient World. Although the statue at Rhodes may be the most famous, the ancient world was home to hundreds of other colossi, such as the chryselephantine statue of Athena at the Parthenon. The Colossus of Rhodes stood for fifty-six years until it was toppled by an earthquake, and it lay in ruins until the

mid-seventh century A.D., when it was sold for scrap. The Colossus of Rhodes and its massive counterparts in antiquity still loom within the English language, however, in the words *colossal* and *coliseum.*)

There may be a faint trace of the Greek word for "rose" in the name of the smallest U.S. state, *Rhode Island.* A sixteenth-century Italian explorer venturing into Narragansett Bay reported that an island there was approximately the size of the Greek island of Rhodes. A century later, Dutch settlers observed the red clay on this island's shore and began to call it *Rood Eiland,* the "red island." Over time each of these ideas, "red" and "Rhodes," apparently reinforced the other.

Finally, Greek *rhodon* is part of the name of the botanical genus *Rhododendron.* This name literally means "rose-tree." Greek *dendron,* or "tree," is also found in the name of the "tree-loving" vine *philodendron,* and in *dendrochronology,* the science of analyzing tree rings to help determine archaeological dates. The *Rhododendron* genus encompasses several shrubs that bear fragrant flowers ranging from white to red. One of these, *oleander,* takes its name from Latin *arodandrum,* which is probably an altered form of *rhododendron.* The "rose-trees" also include the *azaleas,* which are named from the Greek word *azaleos,* "dry," because they are thought to thrive in parched soil. (Greek *azaleos* is kin to such "dry" or "burning" words as *arid, ardor, ardent,* and *arson.*)

· · ·

FROM Greek *rhodon* also comes the Latin word for "rose," *rosa.* Imperial Rome was passionately in love with the rose. During festivals roses were strewn throughout the streets and draped over statues. Revelers sported garlands of roses on their heads and dined while reclining on ornate cushions filled with rose petals, savoring such culinary delights as rose-flavored jellies, puddings, wine, and water. The history of Rome is replete with stories of vast expenditures of money for thousands of roses to decorate a banquet hall for a single evening. The decadent Emperor Heliogabalus was famous for throwing lavish banquets at which guests were showered with rose petals. It is alleged that at one such feast so many petals were dropped from the ceiling that several guests smothered.

ROSE

. . .

Venus, the Romans' goddess of beauty and erotic love, was closely associated with this seductive blossom. *Mea rosa,* or "my rose," was a term of endearment. According to some myths, Venus caused the rose's red color when she pricked her foot on the thorn of a white rose, and her blood fell upon its blossoms. Other stories say her son, Cupid, spilled some red wine on the white rose, staining it forever.

In yet another myth, Cupid gave a rose to the god of silence, Harpocrates, in return for keeping quiet about Venus's romantic indiscretions. This story is said to have inspired the Latin phrase *sub rosa,* or "under the rose," which describes something to be kept confidential. In modern English both *sub rosa*

161

and its literal translation, "under the rose," still describe this situation. These phrases were given physical, literal interpretations as well. For many years it was fashionable for plasterwork ceilings in European dining rooms to feature a rose motif, assuring guests that their host intended to keep their conversation private. And, beginning in the Middle Ages, a wood carving of a rose was placed in the space over confessional doors in Catholic churches, a subtle guarantee that any sins confessed "under the rose" would be held in strict confidence.

A whiff of Latin *rosa* remains in several other English terms as well. The word *roseola,* for example, means a "rose-colored rash." The image of a "rosy rash" may also be the source of the familiar nursery rhyme "Ring Around the Rosie," one version of which goes:

> Ring-a-ring-o' rosies,
> A pocket full of posies,
> A-tishoo! A-tishoo!
> We all fall down!

Some folklorists believe that this seemingly nonsensical song had its origin in a euphemistic description of the plague, which began with a rosy rash, followed by sneezing and finally death. The "posies" supposedly refers to the herbs that people carried in hopes of warding off the disease.

Similarly, in sixteenth-century England, *the Rose*

was a popular term for an inflammatory or "rosy" skin disease, often accompanied by high fever, also called *St. Anthony's Fire,* after the saint who supposedly had the power to cure it. A more poetic ailment —and certainly a more benign one—is a *rose fever,* also called a *rose cold,* which is simply another name for "hay fever occuring in spring or early summer."

ROSE

· · ·

THE rose appears throughout Christian iconography, which led to the creation of a few other "rose" words. The rose is closely associated with the Virgin Mary—sometimes called the "Rose Without Thorns"—in keeping with the longstanding tradition of linking this flower with various female figures in religion. Thus a Gothic cathedral's *rose window* is identified with the Virgin, and the prayer-counting device called a *rosary* is said to represent the Virgin's "Crown of Roses." (In German, a "wreath" or "garland" is a *Kranz,* and thus a German rosary is a *Rosenkranz.*)

The name of the herb *rosemary* would seem to reflect this link between the most perfect of flowers and the purest of women in Christian tradition. Actually, however, this is another instance of folk etymology at work. The name *rosemary* is a corruption of Latin *ros marinus,* or "sea dew," from the fact that this minty herb grows wild on the sea cliffs of southern Europe. (The *marinus* in *rosemary* is kin to such *marine* words as *maritime, mermaid,* and *marinate,* the process of soaking something in a briny solution.

163

Latin *ros* is the source of English *roscid* and *rorid,* both obsolete words that mean "dewy," and *roriferous,* or "dew-generating." *Ros* is also in the name of the alcoholic cordial *rosolio,* once routinely flavored with the plant botanists call *ros solis,* or the "sundew." This drink is now flavored with sugar, orangeblossom water, raisins, cinnamon, cloves, and rose petals.)

THE ancient Persians were as ardent as the Greeks and Romans in their romance with the rose. In Persian legend, roses grew from beads of sweat that fell from the forehead of Muhammad. The rose is also closely associated with the nightingale in Persian lore; it was said that when the nightingale first saw a white rose she rushed to embrace it and pierced her breast on its thorns. From her blood came the world's first red rose.

The ancient Persians' word for "rose" is *gul,* a name that is related, surprisingly enough, to Greek *rhodon* and Latin *rosa.* The word *gul* is thought to derive from the ancient root **WROD-** via an Iranian form, *wrd,* which underwent a series of regular phonetic changes, by which an initial *w* becomes a *g,* and a final *rd* becomes an *l.* In much of modern Iran the word *gul* is still used to mean "rose." The Turks borrowed this name as *gül,* and in nearby Azerbaijan a rose is a *kul.*

Persian *gul* was also borrowed into English as the name of a small motif, such as a stylized rose, appearing at regular intervals on oriental carpets. Some speakers of English will be familiar with the word *Gulistan,* the name of one of the greatest classics of Persian literature. It was written by Sa'di, a Persian educated in Baghdad who spent thirty years in exile after the Mongol invasion of his homeland. The *Gulistan,* or "Rose Garden," includes polished, elegant, and often wry stories and reminiscences on such topics as romantic love, aging, the virtues of modesty and gentleness, and on the absurdity of existence itself. Today the word *Gulistan* is also the lyrical name of a village in central Azerbaijan.

ROSE

· · ·

One final Persian offspring of **WROD-** is the word *gulāb,* or "rosewater." From this comes the name of the sweet drink that English speakers call a mint *julep.* Made with sugar, crushed ice, a sprig of mint, and generous portions of bourbon, this refreshing and very potent concoction is the traditional drink of choice at the Kentucky Derby—the annual horse race also known as the "Run for the Roses."

Tulip

*T*he gaily colored *tulip* takes its name from the Turkish word *tülbend,* which means "turban." Traces of this Turkish word are more clearly seen in the Danish word for "tulip," *tulipan,* and its Swedish equivalent, *tulpan.* Turkish *tülbend* also led to the English word *turban,* the origin of which is more obvious in Shakespeare's spelling for this type of headdress, *turband.*[1] The tulip was introduced to Europe from Turkey in the mid-1500s by Augier Ghislain de Busbecq, an ambassador of the Austrian Emperor Ferdinand I. While on a diplomatic mission to the sultan of the Turkish Empire, Busbecq became enchanted with the unusual flowers that grew there in abundance. Although the Turks' traditional name for this flower was *lale,* Busbecq's interpreter joked that the blossom was a *tülbend,* referring to its "turbanlike" shape. When Busbecq brought back several of them for the royal gardens at Vienna, he brought along the more picturesque name as well.

. . . .

[1] Turkish *tülbend* is an adaptation of a Persian word for "turban," *dulband.* The progression from *dulband* to *tülbend* and English *turban* is yet another example of the occasional tendency of "l" sounds to change to "r," and "d" sounds to "t."

The tulip, with its distinctive appearance and exotic origins, soon became one of the most popular flowers in Europe. Nowhere was this more true than in Holland, where the demand for tulips grew so enormous that prices soared, touching off a national craze. Speculators began to invest in tulips much as they invest in stocks today. At one point a single bulb of the *Semper Augustus* variety sold for more than the average Dutch citizen could hope to earn in a lifetime. Another variety, *Viceroy,* was reportedly exchanged for a dozen sheep, four oxen, eight pigs, four barrels of beer, two hogsheads of wine, two barrels of butter, half a ton of cheese, half a dozen loaves of bread, a silver pitcher, a bed, and a suit of clothing. Fortunes were made and lost in a matter of hours. Eventually things got so out of hand that the government had to step in and regulate the market. The tulip frenzy, which lasted from 1634 to 1637, is known today as the *tulipomania.*

THE tulip isn't the only flower named for its resemblance to a turban. Another Turkish word for a specific style of turban, *martagān,* inspired the English flower name *martagon.* Both the tulip and the martagon are members of the Lily family—and the martagon is also known, appropriately enough, as the *turk's-cap lily.*

Quite a few flowers, in fact, are named after various kinds of headwear. For example, the starry white blossoms known as *miterwort* are so named because their seed pods look like a *miter,* the pointed liturgical headdress that resembles two convex shields fastened back to back. (Similarly, the heart's *mitral valve,* which regulates blood flow between the left atrium and left ventricle, is so named because it consists of two triangular flaps that resemble a miter.)

TULIP

· · ·

Miterwort, which is also called *bishop's cap,* belongs to the scientific genus *Mitella,* or in Latin, "little miter." (The flowers in the genus *Mitella* are closely related to another genus called *Tellima,* which includes such flowers as false alumroot. The name *Tellima* is an anagram of *Mitella,* one of several botanical names coined in that way.)

The word *miter,* at any rate, comes from an Indo-European root called **MEI-4,** which means "to tie." Also from this root are *miter's* Greek ancestor, *mitra,* which once served as a broad term that could mean "headband," "belt," "girdle," or "turban." This idea of "tying" is also reflected in the name of the ancient Iranian god *Mithra,* who initially presided over contracts, treaties, mutual obligation, and justice—over those things that "tie" human beings to one another. *Mithra* eventually became a major deity identified with the sun, and his worship, *Mithraism,* became extremely popular throughout the Roman Empire. For some two hundred years, from the second to the fourth centuries A.D., Mithraism was probably the most serious rival of another nascent religion, Christianity. These competing faiths shared

169

some strikingly similar features, including the practices of holy communion and baptism to cleanse sins, the promise of spiritual salvation and everlasting life, and even a story about an escape from a great flood in an ark.

The worship of Mithra also inspired the name of a series of ancient kings in Asia Minor called *Mithridates,* or literally, "gift of Mithra." The most famous of these, Mithridates VI, was a shrewd military leader who was among Rome's most formidable enemies. His conduct, however, was characterized by anything but the kind of justice symbolized by his namesake. He murdered members of his own family, including his mother and his sister, whom he had married in order to retain power. He once ordered the death of every Roman citizen living in his territories—reportedly a massacre of some eighty thousand people in a single day.

Mithridates also was famous for building his immunity to various poisons by ingesting small amounts of them over a long period—a wise strategy for a brutal dictator, of course. His efforts to immunize himself were so successful that later, when faced with an insurrection, Mithridates tried to commit suicide by poisoning himself, but could find no drug potent enough to kill him, and had to ask a soldier to finish the job for him. Mithridates lives on, however, in the English words *mithridatism,* "an induced immunity to poison," *mithridate,* "an antidote," and *mithridatize,* "to build immunity to poison by taking small doses over time."

SPEAKING of poisons, one of the botanical world's most toxic members is *monkshood.* This plant, which resembles a monk's cowl, sometimes goes by the name *helmet flower.* The deadly properties of monkshood also inspired some grisly nicknames, including *wolfsbane, dogsbane,* and in Latin, *pardalianches,* or literally, "panther-strangle."

Monkshood is properly known as *aconite,* a name of uncertain origin. Some say this name arose from Greek *akon,* or "dart," because even a small amount of juice from this plant produces a lethal poison used on arrowheads. The more likely explanation, however, is that *aconite* comes from Greek *akoniti,* "without labor," referring to the speed and efficiency with which this extract kills. *Akoniti* (literally, "without dust," from Greek *a,* "not," and *konis,* "dust") originated in ancient wrestling competitions, in which particularly adept athletes were said to dispatch opponents "without raising any dust." (Greek *konis,* or "dust," by the way, is a linguistic relative of Latin *cinis,* or "ashes," from which comes *incinerate,* as well as *cineraria,* the name of a plant with leaves that are covered with an ashlike fuzz.)

IN addition to the tulip, miterwort, and monkshood, several other flowers are named after various types of headgear. The white or purple blossoms called *petasites* are distinguished by their oversize, round leaves reminiscent of a Greek *petasos,* or "broad-brimmed hat." The messenger gods Hermes and Mercury are usually pictured wearing a *petasos.* This word belongs to a family of "flat" or "spread-out" words, including *pan, petal, expand, patent* ("something spread out in plain view"), and *fathom* ("the length of two arms spread out"). The flowers called petasites are also known as *butter-bur,* apparently because their large, rough leaves were once used as a wrapping for butter.

From the Latin word *pileus,* or "felt cap," comes the name of the tropical plant *pilea,* whose flower resembles one. Its name is kin to that of the *pileated woodpecker.* The Latin word *pileus* was also borrowed whole into English, where it now serves as the technical name for a mushroom's cap, a jellyfish's "umbrella," and a similarly shaped type of cloud. Another flower with a "hat" in its name is the tall, golden Japanese perennial called *kirengeshoma: ki,* "yellow," plus *renge,* "lotus blossom," plus *shoma,* "hat."

Finally, *Mrs. Robb's bonnet* is named for a Mrs. Robb of Liphook, Hampshire, who introduced the flower to England in the 1890s. It's a type of *spurge,* the variety of tropical plants named for their medicinal use as a purgative, from Old French *espurgier,* "to purge." Like the ambassador who fell in love with tulips, Mrs. Robb was traveling in Turkey when she became enchanted with an unfamiliar blossom. She gathered as many of the exotic flowers as she could and brought back the rooted specimens in her hatbox.

TULIP

· · ·

Zinnia

*J*ohann Gottfried Zinn, the German professor of botany for whom the *zinnia* is named, lived only from 1727 to 1759. During his short lifetime, he became not only an accomplished botanist, but also a physician who published the first comprehensive book on the anatomy of the eye. This gifted young scientist is the subject of an amusing story recounted in Mary Durant's charming book *Who Named the Daisy? Who Named the Rose?* It seems that Professor Zinn once ventured deep into the mountains of Mexico to collect botanical specimens. One day while hiking along a lonely path, he chanced upon some purple flowers, the likes of which he'd never seen before. He gathered as many as he could, stuffed them into a sack, and continued on his way. Farther down the road, he was attacked by a gang of thieves, but when they snatched away his precious sack of goods, out spilled only a pile of faded purple blossoms. The bandits surmised that their victim must be an idiot—for who but a fool would be wandering the wilds with a bag of dead flowers?—so they let the poor foreigner go, since they considered it bad luck to harm the feeble-minded.

The brilliant flower that commemorates Professor Zinn sometimes goes by the nickname *youth-and-old-*

age. The origin of this name is unclear. Some say it was inspired by the fact that a zinnia's old blossoms still look new even when younger ones start to open. Others suggest it may reflect the way these flowers tend to bloom profusely before quickly succumbing to autumn frost. Still others say the name may also reflect the contrast between the zinnia's tender blossoms and its stiff, whiskered stems.

Professor Zinn's name, by the way, offers yet another example of the correspondence that so often occurs between the German letter *z* and English *t.* In German, the word *Zinn* means the same thing as the English name of the metal called *tin.*

THE zinnia is only one of many flowers that take their names from the names of actual persons. Indeed, quite a few of the flower names people are often most curious about—the *poinsettia,* the *camellia,* and the *begonia,* for example—came about this way. As you might expect, these flower names hold within them some intriguing bits of history.

The handsomest of the tropical vines, *bougainvillea,* commemorates Louis Antoine de Bougainville, an eighteenth-century French navigator who was also an expert mathematician as well as a scientist, politician, military leader, writer, and explorer. Among other things, Bougainville founded a French colony in the Falkland Islands and led the first French expedition around the world.

Bougainville's memoirs of his South Sea explorations between 1766 and 1769 include the fascinating tale of twenty-six-year-old Jean Baret, an assistant to the naturalist who was traveling with the expedition, an elderly scientist named Philibert de Commerson. Admiral Bougainville wrote that young Baret was "not particularly handsome, but quiet and hardworking." The crew even referred to the young man as Commerson's "beast of burden" because of the remarkable strength and endurance he showed while hauling around all of the naturalist's heavy equipment.

ZINNIA

· · ·

There was just one small problem: The young man assisting the naturalist was actually a young woman. She had desperately wanted to make that journey, but knowing she would never be allowed to join the expedition as a woman, she disguised herself as a man.

Her ruse worked smoothly until they reached Tahiti. There a young chieftain somehow saw through her disguise and tried to carry her off. Baret was rescued by a French officer who happened upon the scene. Next, as author Michael Ross phrased it in his book *Bougainville:*

> One of the soldiers determined by hook or by crook to find out the truth, and his indiscreet curiosity revealed to him without a doubt that [the chieftain] had not been mistaken . . . Now that her

177

secret was out, it was recollected that she had never changed her underclothes in public and no one could remember ever having seen her shave.

Bougainville himself proved relatively understanding about the whole matter, as evidenced by his own writings:

> She knew from the outset the goal that was in prospect, and the idea of such a voyage had excited her curiosity. She would be the first woman to accomplish it and I must do her the justice to acknowledge that at all times while she was on board ship she was the model of propriety.

The admiral went on to note, however, that if the expedition had been shipwrecked on a desert island, "Fate would have played some strange tricks on Baret." As things turned out, Baret (afterward known as Jeanne) was allowed to make the rest of the journey along with the crew and remained the devoted assistant of Commerson until the old man's death a few years later.

The story of Jeanne Baret's restless curiosity—as well as the lengths to which she had to go to satisfy it—calls to mind another flower named after a similarly determined and resourceful woman. The diminutive blossom is called *lasthenia,* and it grows along the Pacific coasts of North and South America. This flower honors a young woman of ancient Greece named Lasthenia, who is said to have dressed as a boy in order to attend classes taught by none other than Plato himself.

ZINNIA
. . .

THE festive *poinsettia* is named after a United States politician, Joel Roberts Poinsett. A fervent liberal, Poinsett served in several diplomatic posts during the early nineteenth century and became notorious in several Latin American countries for his insistent meddling in their domestic affairs. As U.S. special agent in Latin American countries then still under Spanish rule, Poinsett initiated diplomatic and commercial relations with them while simultaneously helping their fledgling revolutionary forces. He later served as U.S. minister to Mexico, where he also became deeply involved in local politics. He grew so meddlesome, in fact, that the Mexicans coined the word *poinsettismo* to mean "high-handed, intrusive activity."

Poinsett was also involved in his own country's domestic affairs: He served in Congress and as secretary of war for President Martin Van Buren, and helped establish one of the organizations that would later become the Smithsonian Institution.

Sometime during the 1820s Poinsett, who was also something of a botanist, returned from Mexico with a showy flower which he helped to popularize. The Mexicans called it *la flor de nochebuena* or "Christmas Eve flower," and the British called it *Mexican flameleaf*. In the United States, however—perhaps

with the help of a little *poinsettismo*—this flower that is now a Yuletide favorite honors Poinsett himself.

THE *begonia* commemorates another government official, a seventeenth-century Frenchman named Michel Bégon, who supervised a French colony in the Caribbean. There he pursued the study of botany in his spare time and eventually brought back to Europe the plant that now bears his name. Bégon is also remembered for his love of learning and great public-spiritedness. Among other things, Bégon opened his valuable private library to the public, responding to friends' skepticism about such a venture with the statement: "I had much rather lose my books than seem to distrust an honest man."

CAMELLIAS preserve within their name the memory of a Moravian Jesuit priest named Georg Josef Kamel, who in the early eighteenth century managed a pharmacy for the poor in the Philippines. Kamel kept his pharmacy supplied by cultivating an herb garden and wrote about his botanical findings under the name Camellus, the Latinized version of his real name—Latinizing one's name being a trendy thing to do in those days. The camellia, a close relative of the tea plant, honors this priest-botanist.

In German, by the way, *Kamel* means "camel." The *Georg* in the botanist's name is interesting, too:

Georg and English *George* come from a Greek word meaning "farmer," or literally, "earth-worker." This Greek term, *geōrgos,* is kin to such "earth" words as *geography, geology, geode,* and *georgic* ("pertaining to rural life"). The latter part of this Greek term is related to such "working" words as *energy, synergy, ergonomics,* and *surgery,* the last of which comes from a Greek word that literally means "hand-work." And, we might as well add that the name *Josef* (as in Georg Josef Kamel) and its English counterpart, *Joseph,* come from a Hebrew word meaning "he adds."

ZINNIA
· · ·

FINALLY, one more flower that commemorates a person: the *linnea.* Also known as the *twinflower* because its blossoms appear in pairs, this plant was named by the eighteenth-century Swedish botanist Carl von Linné, better known by his Latinized name, Linnaeus. It was Linnaeus who developed the modern system of scientific classification of plants and animals by assigning them Greek and Latin names.

Linnaeus was reportedly a person of great charm. In the summertime he conducted enormously popular nature walks through the Swedish countryside. The crowds who attended were divided into groups led by Linnaeus and his students, who led them through the fields in search of wildflowers. Whenever the great scientist decided to stop and discourse about a certain flower, the other groups were summoned to the site with French horns played by musicians who went along on those walks for just that purpose.

Linnaeus was also notoriously egotistical, but curiously enough, out of the hundreds of flowers he knew so well, chose one of the humblest to bear his own name. The scientist described the linnea as "a plant of Lapland, lowly, insignificant, disregarded, flowering but for a brief space—from Linnaeus who resembles it."

LIST OF FLOWERS

Flowers in boldface are the subjects of full chapters.

Aconite 171

Alyssum 91

Antholyza 91

Amaranth 10

Amaryllis 3

Anthurium 9

Aster 18

Azalea 160

Begonia 180

Belladonna 8

Belladonna lily 8

Bishop's cap 169

Bougainvillea 176

Butter-bur 172

Butterfly pea 138

Calla lily 104

Calliopsis 104

Calopogon 104

Camellia 180

Capuchine capers 131

Chrysanthemum 27

Cineraria 171

Clematis 75

Clitoria 138

Coleus 137

Columbine 32

Coreopsis 104

A GARDEN
OF
WORDS
• • •

Corn rose	151
Cranesbill	68
Culverwort	35
Cupid's delight	146
Daffodil	83
Daisy	45
Dandelion	59
Day lily	99
Deadly nightshade	8
Dogsbane	171
Dogstones	136
Easter lily	105
Edelweiss	63
Flower-with-a-face	146
Fool's stones	136
Fool's ballocks	136
Foxstones	136
Geranium	66
Gladiolus	72
Gladdon	78
Hare's ballocks	136
Heal-dog	91
Heartsease	146
Helmet flower	171
Hemerocallis	103
Herb Margaret	58
Herb trinity	146
Hippeastrum	4
Hosta	105
Hyacinth	79
Hydrangea	85
Iris	93

Johnny-jump-up 146
Jump-up-and-kiss-me 146
Kirengeshoma 172
Kiss-me 146
Kiss-me-at-the-garden-gate 146
Kiss-me-quickly 146
Lasthenia 178
Leontopodium 63
Lily 98
Linnea 181
Lion's tooth 60
Live-forever 31
Loosestrife 108
Love-in-idleness 146
Lupine 113
Lythrum 112
Madonna lily 101
Madwort 91
Margaret 58
Margaret's herb 58
Martagon 168
Mexican flameleaf 179
Miterwort 168
Monk's head 65
Monkshood 171
Mrs. Robb's bonnet 172
Nasturtium 124
Oleander 160
Orchid 133
Orpine 31
Pansy 141
Penny bean 114

A GARDEN
OF
WORDS
• • •

Petasites 172
Pilea 172
Plantain lily 104
Poinsettia 176
Poppy 149
Rhododendron 160
Rose 157
Rosemary 163
St. Valentine's flower 146
Satyrion 135
Soldier's cullions 137
Spurge 172
Stinking iris 78
Storksbill 68
Sweet cods 136
Sword lily 78
Three-faces-under-a-hood 146
Tickseed 51
Tiger lily 106
Tulip 166
Turk's-cap lily 168
Twinflower 181
Vanilla 137
Violet 148
Wolfsbane 171
Wolf's bean 114
Youth-and-old-age 175
Zinnia 174

ACKNOWLEDGMENTS

*B*ouquets to the many folks who contributed to this book at various points along the way. I'd like to thank in particular:

The University of Kentucky Department of Classical Languages and Literature, especially Hubert Martin, Jr., and Louis Swift.

My mentors and occasional colleagues on the editorial board of the Louisville *Courier-Journal* for sharing their support, encouragement, and lively ideas during the writing process.

My cohorts in the rock band Yer Girlfriend— Carol Kraemer, Kathy Weisbach, Laura Shine, Phyllis Free, our manager Angie Mattingly, sound engineer Sheila Hunley, and especially Patty O. Veranda —for their consistent support and indulgence, and for helping me keep track of all those file cards on road trips.

Wayne Barnette, who read the manuscript and made many invaluable suggestions.

Patty Wren Smith, resident naturalist at Hopscotch House in Prospect, Kentucky, who generously spent countless hours introducing me to the real-life flowers that until then had been only names in books.

My dear friend and colleague Robin Garr, for in-

ACKNOWLEDGMENTS
. . .

valuable technical assistance, writerly support, and synergy.

My editor, Ruth Fecych, for her wise counsel and patience, and Margaret Wimberger, for thorough, sharp-eyed copyediting.

My agent, Gail E. Ross, and Hugh O'Neill, for his initial help in shaping the concept for this book.

I'd like to say a special thanks to my parents for their loving support in encouraging me to follow my curiosity—no matter *where* it leads.

Thanks also to the following individuals for their help: Grace Akers, Tracie Anderson, Mary C. Bingham, Marie Bunce, Sue Carroll, Raoul Clem, the GP, Mary Gurnavage, Sandy Hayden, Oriana Castillo Silva, Anne Hogan, Jo Ann Hughes, Doris M. Jones, the Latkovski family, Fiona McEwan, Julia McGrew, Susan Reigler, Dean Robertson, my friends at St. Francis High School, Adele Scafuro, Laurel Shackelford, Kay Turner, Lindsy Van Gelder, Annie Veranda, Felton Veranda, T. Alvin Veranda, and Deborah Weiner.

And especially to my *sine qua non,* Louisville artist Debra Clem.

Louisville, Kentucky
January 1992